'There is no wealth but life'

(John Ruskin, *Unto This Last*, 1862;
Penguin Classics edition, 1985)

This book is in honour of Dr James Niven
(Medical Officer of Health for Manchester, 1894–1922)
and of all who have worked for the health of the city.

Contents

Acknowledgements

G IVEN THE COMPLEXITY OF OUR STORY and the rapidity of organisational change in Manchester, gathering material for this project has not been easy. That it has finally taken shape is due to the help of many people.

Dr Rajan Madhok initiated the project. He wanted to discover where the leadership for public health in Manchester had been since 1945, and what it had achieved. We would like to thank him for giving us the opportunity to record this history. We hope we have been able to answer some, if not all, of his concerns. But responsibility for the text rests solely with the authors.

The work has been carried out in the Wellcome Unit of the Centre for the History of Science, Technology and Medicine at the University of Manchester, and we are grateful to the Director of the Centre, Prof. Michael Worboys, for his support and encouragement. We are also indebted to the Wellcome Trust for their funding of the Unit, and to them and the Faculty of Life Sciences for a Wellcome Trust VIP award to Emma which assisted the later stages of our work.

The majority of our primary evidence was obtained from interviews. We thank all those listed in the Appendix who gave up their time to share their experiences of *doing* public health in Manchester, and without whom this work would not have been possible.

For their help in providing access to other relevant material, we would like to thank the staff of the Manchester Local Studies Library and Archives, the archivists and librarians at the John Rylands University Library of Manchester, Lynda McKean of the Office of the President and Vice-Chancellor, at the University of Manchester, the staff of the Manchester PCT Library, Neil Bendel of the Manchester Joint Health Unit, and Saleem Zaidi of the Manchester Public Health Development Service. Angela Young was an invaluable source of information and encouragement throughout, and handed over a substantial amount of material from her own personal archive. Dr Christine Hallet, Val Harrington, Dr Elizabeth Toon, Dr Stephanie Snow and Dr Helen Valier all kindly shared the findings of their own research on various aspects of the health services in Manchester. We would also like to thank Christina Ireland, Research and Development Manager, Manchester PCT, for her assistance throughout the project.

Finally, thanks are due to those who took time from their busy schedules to read and comment on various drafts. For this we would particularly like to thank Dr John Ashton, Joanna Baines, Prof. Virginia Berridge, Prof. Sir Robert Boyd, Dr Sally Bradley, Dr Michael Brown, Prof. Stephen Harrison, Prof. Richard Heller, Prof. Robert Millward, Gary Raphael, Dr Stephanie Snow, Dr Elizabeth Toon, Dr John Welshman, Prof. Michael Worboys and Angela Young.

We are grateful to all who have helped, but they are not to be blamed for any faults or opinions in the text. These are ours, and we will be happy to discuss them.

List of Figures

List of Tables

Foreword

One day I walked with one of these middle-class gentlemen into Manchester. I spoke to him about the disgraceful unhealthy slums and drew his attention to the disgusting condition of that part of town in which the factory workers lived. I declared that I had never seen so badly built a town in my life. He listened patiently and at the corner of the street at which we parted company he remarked: 'And yet there is a great deal of money made here. Good morning, Sir!'

Friedrich Engels, The Condition of the Working Class in England (first English Edition, 1887).

WHEN I CAME TO WORK in Manchester in 2005, I began to wonder whether things had really changed in the one hundred and fifty years since Engels wrote the above recollection. Manchester had the lowest life expectancy for men and fourth lowest for women, there were wide health inequalities and the city ranked second in the deprivation league table nationally, and yet there were many highly acclaimed institutions and individuals. So, on the face of it, it appeared that money and reputations were still being made in the City but perhaps its citizens were not reaping the benefits.

I began to wonder why there was such a disparity. Having moved from the 'History is bunk' camp of my youth, I now believe that 'Those who do not learn from history are doomed to repeat the mistakes' and so I talked to my friend John Pickstone at The University of Manchester's Wellcome Unit for the History of Medicine. I asked him about leadership in this field since World War Two: was I being too hard, did anyone come forward to improve the public's health, what did they achieve and what can be learnt from their efforts? These enquiries led to the work presented here.

My personal knowledge about leadership for public health in Manchester, I have to confess, had been limited and also not very positive, at that time. Like other public health professionals in England

I had witnessed, with some alarm, the difficulties in recruiting or retaining senior public health staff and was saddened professionally when for many years in the 1990s, the city refused to appoint a director of public health or a professor of public health.

From the work done by Emma Jones and John Pickstone it seems clear to me that many individuals rose to the challenge and made significant inroads; but they were handicapped by institutional relationships. The three organisations studied here – the local authority, the NHS and the University of Manchester – have rarely moved in common harness, as it were. If we think of three cogs meant to turn a wheel, then only one, or at best two, seem to have been doing the job at any given stage. Sadly, this remains the situation even today: though the relationship between the local authority and the NHS has improved and joint-working has started to produce some tangible results, public health research and teaching in the academic sector now seem to need strengthening.

Manchester, and its historical links with India, has fascinated me from my school days in Delhi. It was a pleasure and a privilege when I finally came to work here. Manchester to me remains the tale of two cities: it is the best of places and it is the worst of places. But there are some grounds to believe that attitudes are changing, and we might look to a renewal of the quest for public health.

From the first industrial city at the start of the industrial revolution to the first world class city in terms of health services, teaching and research in the twenty-first century is a dream worth pursuing, and one that its residents well deserve. If this book plays a part in realizing that breakthrough by supporting and stimulating colleagues and individuals who are working to do so in Manchester, then the effort by Emma and John would have been worthwhile. I am grateful to them for indulging me.

Rajan Madhok
Medical Director, Manchester PCT
Honorary Professor, University of Manchester
Visiting Professor, Manchester Metropolitan University
August 2008

Introduction

To write a history of the quest for 'public health' since the
Second World War is a mighty challenge. Activities related to
public health are diffuse and extend across many agencies; if they
share an overall goal of reducing mortality and morbidity, debate
about priorities and methods persists. Here, we have traced the
histories of services and projects which were labelled as 'public
health', or commonly seen to be so, and we have included statistics
of health in Manchester, together with statistics for other cities and
for England and Wales. Such statistics clearly show the challenges to
public health services; more rarely do they prove their effects.

Ours is largely a history of how the responsibilities and potential
of 'public health' posts were realised by their occupants. Though
some of our stories involve the imaginative creation of new services,
we have also had to chronicle how services were kept going under
circumstances that were difficult – financially and/or in terms of
organisation. Especially since the 1980s, frequent re-organisations of
the NHS (see appendix 3) have proved a major handicap, particularly
in fields such as public health that were closely linked with administrative structures and sometimes seen as less than urgent. Sorting
out a new set of relationships for public health often took second
place to issues around acute medicine, and when new relationships
and responsibilities were finally established, the structures would be
changed yet again.

In the post-war history of Manchester's public health services,
it is not hard to see many difficulties and some declines. The local
authority, Manchester City Council, lost some of its functions to
the new NHS in 1948, and lost several more in the re-organisation
of 1974. The public health functions collected into the main NHS
structures were ill-defined, often marginal and repeatedly disrupted.
In the University, where the Public Health department had boasted
a remarkable array of talent in the 1950s, the following decades saw
more losses than gains, until, at the time of writing, there is no

professor of public health. The Masters Course in Public Health has been subsumed by the National Primary Care Research and Development Centre, which is part of the University of Manchester, but there is little academic focus for helping develop services, or for thinking long term about health standards and medical services – whether in Manchester, Britain, or the world at large.

Of course, the organisation of services is not the issue which most concerns the public, or indeed should most concern historians of 'public health'. We should be more interested in health standards, and since the Second World War, in Manchester as across the West, there have been major gains in life expectancy. Mortality rates have declined, especially for deaths related to birth and maternity, and from the infectious diseases and chronic respiratory diseases which were still important around 1945. Though cancer deaths have remained a major challenge, cardio-vascular deaths among the middle-aged have been lowered. Among the non-fatal diseases, tooth decay has been reduced, and a variety of surgical and pharmaceutical treatments have diminished pain and incapacity from arthritis and other chronic illnesses.

All these are reasons for celebration. Some are due to advances in clinical medicine, especially new treatments; some to clinics and domiciliary visits, especially around childbirth. More are due to improvements in diets and air quality. The maintenance of good water supplies and effective sewage systems continues to protect us from the infectious diseases which are still endemic or epidemic in poorer countries. New challenges such as AIDS have been met and Manchester, as a regional leisure capital with a large gay population, managed the 1980s epidemic at least as well as any other British city. Less visible challenges, including the incidence of tuberculosis in immigrant populations, have also been met, and as we shall see, Manchester was amongst the nation's leaders in the provision of special services for immigrant groups.

So if we want to be sanguine about Manchester's public health, we could continue to rely on this type of comparison over time (rather than between sites). Such comparisons have been positive since about 1860 (and would have been from c.1700 to 1800, had one had access to the mortality statistics which historians have recently put together from parish records). But it was not longitudinal statistics which fired-up public health campaigners in the twentieth century or in the nineteenth.

In the mid nineteenth century, when 'public health' was being constructed as a major social issue, and Manchester was central to the national debate, statistics became a novel form of argument. The newly collected numbers by which people were urged to action usually involved comparisons between areas. What moved campaigners then, and may move them still, is the notion of unnecessary or preventable deaths, assessed, albeit crudely, by comparing poor areas with richer areas. The excess mortality in poor areas was deemed preventable, as it still may be. Manchester, from the 1830s, was notable for excess deaths, and has remained so.

Of course, there were other crucial spurs to action, including the fear that contagions would spread from the poor to the rich, or that high infant mortality and feeble children would weaken the nation; or from worries about growing medical expenditure and the hope that better health education and preventative measures might slow the increase. As we shall see, these public fears proved powerful motors in successive periods: but they all commonly involved some calculation of what could be saved or secured, and those calculations involved estimates of differences between rich and poor. What was the *difference* in infections between districts – the infectious potential, as it were, which threatened more salubrious districts? What was the *excessive* mortality and morbidity which undermined nation and empire? And what, presently, are the sicknesses or risk factors that might be targeted if one hopes to reduce the load on medical services?

When we turn to look at these spatial mortality differences, *between* places, and ask about social equity and cohesion, then Manchester, from the start of public health statistics served as an exemplar of excessive mortality, especially for its industrial districts. In the 1830s and 1840s, Manchester was the 'shock city of the age.' One had only to compare it with a rural county to measure the impact on health of rapid urbanisation. At the time of the Boer War, when Manchester youths volunteered for service, their poor physiques became a national scandal – taken as evidence of racial decline that was especially acute among the industrial working classes. And still Manchester remains paradigmatic for relatively high mortality, low life expectancy (see table 1.1), and for problems such as smoking, poor diets and teenage pregnancy.

Though the rawness of the early industrial city was moderated in the decades before the Great War, the subsequent decline of the old industries created new problems. To some extent, new industries buffered Manchester in the interwar depression, when compared with its satellite industrial towns; and new industries and state investments boosted the regional economy for about 20 years after the war. Social housing, first tried in the 1890s, spread in the 1920s and 1930s and boomed after the Second World War. From the 1980s, central Manchester was reinvented as a post-industrial city, but the 'collar' of social housing and the outlying estates were little affected.

Table 1.1   Life expectancy at birth (in years) in eight major English regional cities, based on mid-year population estimates and numbers of deaths for the period 2003–2005.

Cities	Males (Years)	Female (Years)
Manchester	72.5	78.3
Birmingham	74.8	80.1
Bristol	76.3	80.8
Leeds	76.2	81.2
Liverpool	73.4	78.1
Newcastle upon Tyne	74.9	80.2
Nottingham	73.5	79.3
Sheffield	76.6	80.6
England	76.9	81.1

Source: Manchester Joint Health Unit, *A Picture of Progress: Compendium of Statistics, 2007*.

Indeed the subsidised sale of some council housing to the richer occupants tended to increase the concentration of poorer tenants who had no hope of ownership.

And through all this complex history, health differentials persisted. Manchester now tops the table of English cities for male mortality. (Figure 1.1, compares the most recent trends in male mortality for all causes of death in Manchester and England and Wales.) For over 200 years, for all Manchester's life as a 'great town', differential mortality, both within the city and beyond, has constituted a challenge which has been met more or less actively.

The second chapter of this book surveys public health problems and politics from the time of Manchester's industrialisation in the late eighteenth century, through to the twentieth century and the growth of the welfare state. It runs from fever epidemics around the early mills, to the classical problems of urban health as they appeared c.1830–1870. It looks at the growth of philanthropy and local government action around the end of the nineteenth century, and how the central state adopted many of the innovations when the ruling interests were threatened by the rise of labour, and Britain's economic and military power seemed to depend on the health and strength of the population. These themes are followed through the interwar depressions, and this history serves as the backdrop for the radical changes in public health perspectives, politics and organisation which accompanied the creation of the NHS after the Second World War.

In assessing the history of the post-war period we can gain from

Figure 1.1   Trends in male mortality from all causes of death, Manchester Local Authority, and England and Wales, 1995–2005.

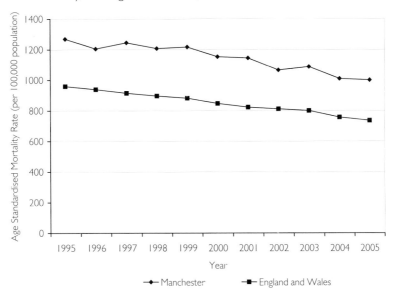

Source: Manchester Joint Health Unit, *A Picture of Progress: Compendium of Statistics, 2007,* and Office of National Statistics datasets from *Health Statistics Quarterly,* 26 (2005), 3C (2006), and 34 (2007).

this longer perspective; we can see how concerns shifted and how a succession of problems were construed and counteracted. We shall see how different groups of people took up these challenges with the methods and instruments of their time. We shall see periods of complacency and distraction as well as activity and innovation. And if some of the six decades since the Second World War seem characterised by disorganisation and dispersion of effort, then a longer perspective may provide alternatives to melancholic extrapolations. We may perhaps learn from history how public heath effort might be renewed.

CHAPTER TWO

From the Industrial Revolution to the Welfare State

Though it is from the 1830s and 1840s that Manchester is best known in the history of public health, the area's prior history is also important.[1] It concerns the initial impacts of industrialisation in the later eighteenth century, when the local responses were mostly through charitable associations rather than statutory action or representations to parliament. To begin our narrative here will connect our urban story with a longer and continuing history of global public health, in which poor harvests and hunger were more important than urban squalor.[2] It will connect us to a prosperous regional capital already known as a centre for trade in textiles that were spun and woven in cottages or small workshops. From 1752, Manchester had boasted an Infirmary, one in a wave of charity hospitals that spread across English county towns and mercantile centres around the mid century. From 1755 it occupied Manchester's grandest new building, in Piccadilly. (Since 1908 the site has been mostly gardens). By the 1780s, the Manchester Infirmary had grown remarkably, including a Lunatic Hospital and Baths for its patients and its subscribers, and some of its surgeons and physicians were nationally known. It was the key institution for attending to 'public health' when the town was challenged by the advent of large scale factories and rapid immigration from the surrounding counties.

Fever and Destitution

The high profile epidemic disease of eighteenth-century Britain was 'fever', specifically the malignant fever (sometimes called typhus) associated with hunger and overcrowding – whether in ships or jails, lodging houses or the hovels of the poor. Fever attained a particular salience around Manchester from c.1780 because it was also associated with new factories built for the spinning of cotton, and deeply resented by those whose domestic work was thereby undercut.[3] Were not factories hot and confined, full of sweaty people and stale air? Did they not generate fever, so compounding economic oppression with epidemic morbidity? And if factories or large workshops attracted migrants, and these migrants packed into lodging houses or cellars, then were not the 'nests of fever' multiplied, rendering the town more dangerous for all its inhabitants?

This challenge to the nascent industrial order was met in part by local physicians, among whom Thomas Percival was most eminent. He was the central figure in a report on fever at a mill near Bury (1784); and in 1802 he again worked with the mill's owner, by then Sir Robert Peel, in an early and largely unsuccessful attempt to regulate child labour in factories. In 1790, Percival was a leader of the reform party in a mammoth political contest at Manchester Infirmary. The issue was the proposed expansion of the honorary staff of the hospital and the extension of the so-called 'Dispensary' service to outpatients and to home patients. The latter often suffered from fever and were attended in the filthy cellars they called home.

The opposition to this extension programme was led by the town's premier surgeon Charles White, who had helped found the Infirmary. White was also well known for his expertise in midwifery, and when the reformers won, he left to found a maternity charity which became St. Mary's.[4] Political dispute had increased the range of charity services.[5]

In 1796 the Infirmary expanded again, by founding a House of Recovery to accommodate fever patients. The Infirmary and its associated charities now formed one of the most extensive medical institutions in Britain. But 1796 was the last big venture. From 1792–1793 the country had been at war with revolutionary France and reformers were under suspicion or outright repression. Thenceforth, the services seem to have been cut back, and the Infirmary settled to being a centre of clinical medicine and education, leaving public health questions to lesser charities.

Manchester in the 1780s and 1790s had responded positively to the increasing threat of fever, not through its statutory government (which was then appropriate only for a village), nor through the machinery of the Poor Law (though the town workhouse was rebuilt in 1793), but by means of its charitable associations, including a Board of Health which was created in 1796 at the same time as the fever hospital, and which attempted to regulate lodging houses and oversee street cleaning, etc.

By any standards, this was a remarkable local initiative: the fever hospital and Board of Health were copied in London, and details were circulated by a national society for 'Bettering the Condition of the Poor'. The expansion was achieved through the co-operation of well-known doctors with local merchants who valued education and civic ventures. Their aim was to maintain health standards in a rapidly growing and controversial town; their chief meeting point was the Unitarian chapel on Cross Street, which combined cool religion with high intellectual and social aspirations. The reformers had led Manchester around 1790, but during the Napoleonic wars they became objects of suspicion. Medical services seem to have been reduced then, and soup kitchens were popularised as a means of feeding the destitute without disturbing the market in grain and bread.

The repression continued after the wars, symbolised by the Peterloo massacre in 1819, when the emergent working classes demonstrated for political rights and the local volunteer cavalry panicked and rode into the crowd. But in the 1820s there were some richer years and new social groups appeared, with novel ways of seeing a considerably expanded city.

Shock Districts

When a new kind of public-health concern appeared in Manchester in the 1830s, it was no longer about the town as a whole: it chiefly concerned new industrial districts such as Ancoats and Chorlton on Medlock (near what became Oxford Rd Station), where enormous mills had been built in the 1790s and extended thereafter. Around the mills were close packed 'cottages' in terraces or courtyards. Ill-built and damp, they had polluted wells for their water supply and relied on dung heaps as the major way of removing human excrement. The contrast between industrial grandeur and domestic squalor became a staple of social commentary through to the mid century, and Manchester in this period had many visitors and commentators. They came to see the future, as later generations would visit New York, or now Shanghai.

By the early 1820s the economy had improved a little. In both the main industrial suburbs, dispensaries were founded by the charitable or the fearful, to provide outpatient and home patient services. Unlike infirmaries, dispensaries had no beds; but many dispensaries grew to become hospitals, some in their early years, some around 1870. Young doctors were often attached to dispensaries on an honorary (unpaid) basis, to help examine the outpatients and visit the home patients. Some of these doctors became the privileged witnesses who documented what became the classic 'public health problems' of industrialization.

The social imagery now was less about air, circulating or stagnant, than about physical and moral decay; about rotting organic matter and rotting people, ready to burst into disease or political agitation should the germs of epidemics (or of political agitation) set light to the tinder. The cholera epidemic of 1831–1832 seemed to prove that model, especially in Manchester which was now the test-case for the nascent and rather British science of political economy.

The Asiatic cholera was understood as a new disease which had spread from India. To most contemporary doctors, its progress was less a matter of a specific contagion than an exotic way of demonstrating which districts of Britain were exceptionally ready for disease. The key Manchester witness was a young physician educated in Edinburgh – James Phillips Kay. He had grown up near Manchester and was already interested in political economy. His friends included young bank staff and merchants, and between them they invented a range of social tools which helped make Manchester central to a national debate.

Manchester, as we have seen, already had a Board of Health and a Fever Hospital. When it was clear epidemic cholera had arrived in the city, the city fathers and medical leaders opened emergency cholera hospitals where victims could be nursed and kept from increasing the menace in their overcrowded houses. There were attempts to clean up the town and posters urged cleanliness and temperance, but Manchester was now more obviously divided by class and 'race' as well as geography; poor Irish immigrants were blamed for exacerbating social problems. The doctors thought themselves newly scientific, but the poor were suspicious of their new fondness for dissection. A major riot erupted at one of the cholera hospitals when a dead child was taken away by Irish relations who then discovered the boy's head had been removed.

The remedies that mid nineteenth-century reformers prescribed for social degeneration were drawn less from medicine than from liberal political economy. To function well, industrial society would require the workers to have a basic education and take responsibility for the future welfare of their families. Workers' own savings were crucial, and missions were invented to spread Providence. For Kay, it was a double pity that the intemperate Irish were spreading bad habits among the natives.

Because they believed that better diagnostic information would facilitate social therapeutics, Kay and his friends founded the Manchester Statistical Society to collect data about education and social conditions. But to most middle-class eyes, the best means to civilise the massed poor, many of whom were young couples away from their parental families, was to preach the Christian gospel. Cleanliness and godliness would be the twin goals in this battle against barbarism – which is how it appeared even to sober commentators.[6]

Kay did not remain a Manchester physician. Partly because of overwork and partly because a major mill owner thought him unsuitable as a son-in-law, he left and became an Assistant Commissioner for the national poor law system. This had been recently reformed along lines suggested by Edwin Chadwick, a 'briefless barrister' who (though born in Manchester) had grown up in London.[7] The reform of the English Poor Law provided the context in which observations like Kay's would achieve a new salience.

Poor Law and Public Health

In England and Wales, from the time of Elizabeth I, the destitute had been entitled to relief payments, drawn from local taxes. After considering the abolition of this statutory relief, so that the poor, as in Scotland, would have to rely on charity, Chadwick decided on a major bureaucratic reform. Parishes would be combined into Poor Law Unions, run by officials who were kept in line through regular reporting and inspections. The operation of the poor law would be 'self-acting', like the new power looms: the poor would look after themselves unless they were utterly desperate, when they could get state support by entering workhouses. But the workhouse accommodation and food were to be so basic and the regimes so hard, at least for the able-bodied, that no-one would choose that institutional life if they had any real alternative.

The threat of this kind of workhouse hung over the poor through Victoria's long reign and, to a lesser degree, until after the Second World War. After c.1870, workhouse hospitals were created as a solution to the problem of chronic illness among the destitute – but they were not common until the end of the century and were not generous with comforts. The New Poor Law also proved a key context for major public debates about public health.

When Chadwick and assistants such as Kay implemented the New Poor Law, they were primarily aiming to reduce the cost of poverty to the state. They wanted to force a division between the hopelessly destitute in institutions and the rest of the poor in the open market for labour. That most inhabitants of poorhouses were in fact incapacitated by disability, disease or age, was not central to the model.

Nor were reformers thinking of the fluctuations of agricultural productivity, which had been so central to poverty and health throughout the eighteenth century and which returned in the mid

1840s when the potato crop failed in Ireland for two successive years. Manchester (though less than Liverpool or Glasgow) then felt the impact of emigrant poverty and fever, adding to the depression of industry.

Accounts of poverty and welfare in industrial towns have often also missed the fact that industry too was cyclical, with major booms and busts, radically changing the price of labour and possibilities of work. That was one of the reasons why the New Poor Law was resisted in industrial Lancashire – not so much in the largest towns such as Manchester, which had a substantial middle class and a growing variety of industries, but in less varied, largely working-class towns such as Oldham, where the New Poor Law became one of the persistent grievances of the working classes.

The Poor Law administration in such towns had already been efficient in bureaucratic terms, but recognised that much of the poverty was due to trade depressions over which workers had no control. Treating such unemployment as a moral failure was as impractical as it was unjust; in times of severe trade depression there had to be some scope for 'out-relief'.

It was mid century before the New Poor Law was fully instituted in Lancashire, by which time Chadwick and his colleagues had moved the agenda from poor relief to matters of health.[8] If poor rates were not being wasted on the undeserving, or in supplementing agricultural wages, then why were there still so many paupers who could not be deterred? One answer was disease – either of the paupers themselves, or by the sickness or death of 'breadwinners'. Which brought reformers back, with new energy, to one of the key questions of the day – why did the poorer districts of towns seem to generate so much disease?

The early enquiries of Kay and the Manchester Statistical Society helped prompt investigations, and around 1840 Chadwick launched a national enquiry on the health of towns. The causes for sickness then suggested by witnesses and local correspondents were many and varied, both moral and physical. They usually included lack of education, want of temperance, overwork, and pitiful housing, as well as poor food, dirty water, and minimal sanitation. But Chadwick directed the conclusions towards the causes he saw as remediable.

He adopted peculiar medical theories from his radical medical friends, who linked disease in British slums with military and colonial experience of tropical fevers and malaria. They saw disease as generated by rotting matter, including the fevered bodies of existing sufferers. In this respect, the slums of Manchester resembled the swamps of Africa – but the slums could be cleansed if pure water was piped in and sewage piped out. Here was a simple if expensive remedy, one which many doctors and other would-be reformers saw as narrow and simplistic. Chadwick's remedies, however, chimed with other reasons for engineering water supplies.[9] Manchester factory owners wanted clean water for their mills, and water under pressure also proved useful for extinguishing the factory and warehouse fires which were a common hazard to business. The better engineering of drains would reduce the frequent floods when rivers over-spilled into low-lying areas of industry and poor housing. And cleaning up the areas of town travelled by the better classes would improve amenities for inhabitants and visitors alike.

Manchester Corporation, set up through the national reforms of the 1830s which spread electoral power to the middle classes, was dominated by industrialists and merchants. From the 1840s, they built a series of reservoirs in Longdendale, engineered by John Frederick La Trobe Bateman. By mid century, clean water from the Pennine moors was being piped into commercial premises and larger houses, but not into the homes of the poor; they were provided with stand-pipes and taps in the courtyards or at the ends of terraces. Though drains were improved in the centre of towns and measures were taken to avoid flooding, there was no major programme to remove sewage from poorer districts. Some of the excrement washed into surface drains, some mixed into the foul earth, and much was piled at depots on the edge of town where farmers could collect it on their way back from the town's markets. Not until c.1870 were the poorer districts cleaned-up, and not till the end of the century by clean water. Over the century, and especially in the late 1860s and early 1870s, national legislative powers were extended; but local implementation usually depended on local complaints and

Table 2.1 Average annual crude mortality rates (per 1000 population) per decade, Manchester, Salford, Liverpool, and Birmingham registration districts, 1841–1900.

	1841–50	1851–60	1861–70	1871–80	1881–90	1891–1900
Manchester*	33.08	31.48	32.80	32.16	29.09	28.29
Salford	27.66	26.00	26.89	27.65	24.72	24.28
Liverpool	-	-	-	33.57	33.13	33.20
Birmingham	-	-	-	25.82	23.00	24.10

* The deaths from 1871–80 relate to the District of Manchester, as constituted after the separation of the Union of Prestwich on 1st October 1874.
Source: General Register Office, Annual Report of the Registrar-General of Births, Deaths and Marriages in England and Wales. Decennial Supplements, 1871–1900, and M. E. Pooley and C. G. Pooley, 'Health, Society and Environment in Victorian Manchester', in R. Woods and J. Woodward (eds), Urban Disease and Mortality in Nineteenth Century England (London, 1984), pp.148–175.

investment. Over such matters there was continual conflict between 'economisers' and reformers; the former opposed what they saw as unnecessary expenditure, the latter focussed on preventable deaths and morbidity.[10]

Mid Century Reports and Societies

The cholera epidemic, Kay's book, and a series of reports helped create a major social issue – the Condition of England. It was to enter international politics in the work of Friedrich Engels, a young German merchant who drew on his life in Manchester to publicise the appalling conditions created by the new urban industry. Nationally, the Health of Towns Association pushed for sanitary legislation, which, after a series of new reports, was realised in the Public Health Act of 1848. It also promoted the official inspection of many smaller towns and the provision of better water and sewage, though this would sometimes take decades to accomplish.

Though Liverpool appointed its own Medical Officer of Health (MOH) in 1847, Manchester Council saw no need. Their waterworks were under construction and the city's engineers knew about drains, so why appoint a 'doctor for the dead'? Since its foundation in 1838, the City Council was keen on remunerative civic utilities, including the gas supply, and its waterworks became a model for other cities worldwide; but it was not notable for attention to health.

Locally, the push for public health was taken up by a voluntary society, the Manchester and Salford Sanitary Association (MSSA), a mix of laymen and doctors who argued for more legislation and especially for better documentation of health conditions. This group collected its own statistics on epidemic disease, and its interest in health education helped originate a Ladies Sanitary Association (LSA) which sent working-class health visitors into the homes of the poor.

The MSSA and LSA formed a key node in a network of middle-class philanthropists which grew substantially by the end of the century. Some groups took up the support of hospitals, and perhaps their reform – a cause boosted by the Crimean work of Florence Nightingale. One of Nightingale's allies in Manchester was John Roberton, a Scottish surgeon and man-midwife who gave his services to the maternity charity and had long been a critic of the Manchester Infirmary.[11] Though the Infirmary buildings had been remodelled around mid century, when the Lunatic hospital moved to Cheadle and the Fever Hospital's functions had passed partly to the workhouse, the structure did not have the cross-ventilation advocated by Roberton; in the morning the wards smelt.

From about 1870 onwards, some surgeons sprayed their operating theatres with carbolic, the antiseptic advocated by Joseph Lister and often used to de-odorise sewage. Carbolic was made in Manchester by Crace Calvert, a manufacturing chemist who also put it into tooth powder. Here was a very industrial substitute for cleanliness, for carbolic was a by-product of the gas industry; even the rubber sheets used to protect against the spray were made in Manchester by Macintosh. Indeed, Manchester was then well known for its expert chemists, several of whom took an interest in public health, including industrial pollution and the components of foul air – particulate or gaseous – which were suspected of causing disease. By the early 1870s, the academic chemist Henry Roscoe had established the new 'Owens College' as a centre of chemical education and research. Roscoe helped the College to incorporate the Manchester Medical School, the latest in a series of medical schools owned by doctors, which since 1817 had educated local medical students not rich enough to go to Edinburgh or London.[12]

Owens College, which became a University college in the 1880s, fed new blood into existing middle-class philanthropic networks. Roscoe, for example, was a great populariser of science, and we shall see at the end of the century how medical scientists at the college began to shape public health questions. Though these questions were rarely central ones for the medical school, the Infirmary, or local medical professional bodies, several individual doctors contributed importantly to the MSSA or related philanthropic organisations campaigning to improve the welfare of the working classes.

Some reformers focussed on education, including the problems of hungry children, or those whose mental or physical handicaps seemed to make them unfit for the primary schools they were supposed to attend after the introduction of universal primary education in 1870. Some concentrated on physical education in schools, and in lad's clubs set up in working-class districts to promote responsibility and reduce crime.

The attack on alcohol through promotion of abstinence was another major focus of social action. Band of Hope classes attached to many dissenting churches worked hard to keep young people out of public houses, and Temperance Associations provided an alternative form of sociability. Temperance also shaded into various other health movements, such as herbalism and vegetarianism, of which Manchester was a stronghold.[13]

All these reform activities were 'voluntary', a matter of local associations supported mostly by the lower middle classes, and by some of the upper working classes, who now had a little leisure time and spare money. They mixed self-improvement with a concern for others. They also exemplified the liberal belief that social problems could best be solved outside government.

Indeed, the MSSA in some ways substituted for a Medical Officer of Health until as late as 1868, when the council appointed John Leigh. But this was hardly a great leap forward. Leigh was a local practitioner and an expert chemist, but not well known among health reformers. He managed, however, to close the remaining cellar dwellings, and succeeded in drawing attention to the high rate of mortality among children – a fact which had been well known but hitherto treated as part of the problem of general mortality. The MSSA wanted municipal provision of an infectious disease hospital, but Monsall Hospital (in north Manchester) was provided as a gift from Robert Barnes, a great supporter of the Infirmary, and it was initially operated as a branch of the Infirmary. By about 1870, as some of the worst housing was removed, often by clearances for new railways or streets, and as clean water became more available, so the problem of infectious disease seemed to shift – away from poorly differentiated fevers seen as saturating putrid districts, towards more differentiated diseases, some of which were characteristic of childhood.

Leigh did not favour the wholesale provision of a water-carriage sewage system, though Chadwick had advocated such a system in the

Pail closet removal, Water Street Yard, Manchester, 1901.

© MANCHESTER LIBRARIES.

1840s. It seemed impractical in Manchester even in the 1860s, when national legislation forced attention to sewage removal. Whereas cities like London, Liverpool or Glasgow were on large rivers close to the sea, Manchester was 30 miles inland. Its rivers were small and already highly polluted, and they flowed through other well-populated areas before reaching the sea. So, when pushed to create a sewage system, Manchester's leaders chose to invest in 'dry-closet' privies, from which buckets of night soil were collected on special wagons, which brought clean buckets in return. The night soil went to a huge depot in Beswick, with its own canal and railway sidings. The initial plan was to convert human excrement into agricultural matter, and the Beswick works did indeed sell fertiliser. But the importation of guano (accumulated bird-excrement) from South America had lowered the price of fertiliser and the sewage work never made a profit. Much of the excrement went unprocessed to be spread on 'moss land'. In the late nineteenth century, Manchester Council owned a large area of farmland to the west of the city which was let out to small holders who agreed to take a set amount of excrement each year.[14]

Late Victorian and Edwardian Social Politics

By the last decade of the century, Britain's politics had changed considerably from the political settlements of the 1830s. In cities like Manchester, the mill owners and merchants no longer held all the reins of government. Many of the leading wealthy families had left town, perhaps to cease active concern with business, perhaps to commute from Alderley Edge or the like. Working men had the vote from 1868, and political parties were developed to mobilise their support and to head-off the threat of more direct representation of labour interests, which by the 1890s was a real possibility. One reason for the rapid development of charity hospitals in industrial towns was their ability to bring together social classes and religious groups in a common cause – and one associated with Nightingale nursing and moral discipline. Especially after 1900, the existing political parties sought working-class support through the extensions of welfare measures such as old-age pensions, often copied from Germany where they had been invented for much the same reasons, albeit in a less democratic polity.

In terms of global economics, Britain's industrial supremacy was being challenged by Germany and by the rapid development of the United States. By the 1890s, Britain was becoming defensive in many senses. Militarisation, technical education and better welfare provision became popular causes, as contributions to 'national efficiency'.[15]

Reformers stressed the need for a large and healthy population. Where the early nineteenth century had worried about excess population and poor relief, the generations around 1900 worried about the falling birth rate in the middle classes and the waste of life through persistently high infant-mortality. As figures 2.1 and 2.2 indicate, mortality for most age groups was falling in the last decades of the nineteenth century, but infant mortality actually rose in towns such as Manchester, declining only from the early 1900s.

Many of the reform measures passed by the national government after 1900 had been pioneered from the 1870s, and especially the 1890s, in the voluntary associations we have just mentioned. The 'strengthening of the state' was often realised through an incremental take-over of voluntary activities by local government, and Manchester became prominent in this movement.[16] The Council was also backing schemes to boost the economy by massive investment in infrastructure. Annual sanitary expenditure increased during the 1870s, much of it invested in improvements to the pail-closet system and to the collection and disposal of night soil. But the major surge in capital formation in sanitation started in the 1890s when Manchester finally began conversion to a water-carriage system of sewage disposal.[17] Annual local taxation returns reveal that expenditure on sewerage and sewage disposal works in the City rose from c. £11,700 in 1888–1889

Figure 2.1   Death rates (per 1000 persons) in specific age groups in Manchester, 1871–1880* to 1891–1900.

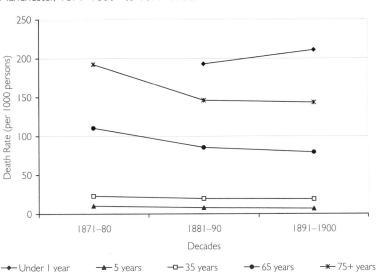

Source: Registrar General's Decennial Supplements, 1871–1900.
* The deaths here relate to the District of Manchester, as constituted after the separation of the Union of Prestwich on 1st October 1874.

Figure 2.2 Death rates (per 1000 persons under 1 year) in specific age groups in Manchester, 1901–1931.

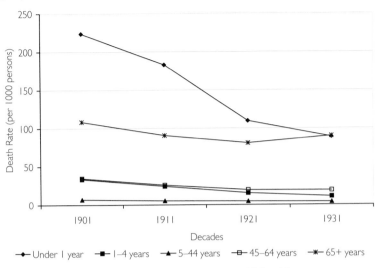

Source: *Health Inequalities and Manchester* (Manchester, 1986), p.33.

to £112,858 in 1890–1891. Expenditure on water works increased from c. £89,000 to £460,792 in the same period. Manchester was also digging a ship canal to allow ocean traffic to bypass Liverpool docks. That scheme had implications for sewage, and so did the plan to supplement the Longdendale water supply by converting a Lake District lake into a municipal reservoir. Providing new infrastructure on this scale, including extensions of gas supply and the installation of electricity, also meant that Manchester Council became a major supplier of utilities to the immediate suburbs – which were thereby drawn into the City as part of a huge new municipality.[18]

The promotion of public works such as these in the 1890s attracted working-class support as well as that of businessmen. The ship canal was an especially popular cause, and there was strong working-class support for the clearance of slums, and then for social housing. Public anger about the condition of privies, especially in Ancoats, had been mobilised by Charles Rowley, a follower of Ruskin and briefly a member of the City Council.[19] His views were supported by a detailed report by Dr J. C. Thresh (sponsored by the MSSA) which systematically demolished the claims made for the dry-closet system.[20] Even if the householders followed all the instructions and covered their excrement with ashes from their domestic fires, the privies still did not work as had been claimed.[21]

For the reformers of Ancoats, however, this critique of sanitation was but a part of the anger and the hope. From the 1890s through to the First World War, the Ancoats district was a focus for social reformers, some of whom had grown up there, whilst some were richer folk exercising favourite schemes for uplift. Edwardian Ancoats had an art gallery for the workers and a University Settlement where Manchester University students could mix with the locals and help organise a wide range of instructional and inspirational activities. Rowley ran a series of high quality lectures and recitals which featured the likes of George Bernard Shaw, the literary critic and playwright, and Prince Kropotkin, the Russian anarchist and high priest of mutualism.[22] The politics were socialistic, but with the Ruskinian stress on art and the enrichment of common life. Remember here Ruskin's motto for his critique of industrial capitalism: there is no wealth but life.

The combination of business interest and working-class agitation meant that by 1900 sanitation in Manchester had moved up a gear,

Housing and water closets at 2 Stone Street, Ancoats, 1897.

© MANCHESTER LIBRARIES.

at least in principle. Practice might take longer because conversion was a major undertaking, but instead of standpipes on the street, all houses were to have a tap in the back kitchen. The front room, which tended to open directly onto the street, was usually gas-lit, with a Lancashire range where a coal fire also heated an oven and kettles. In the backyard, the privy would now have a water closet, and a dustbin. Terraces built at the end of the century usually had a corridor from the front door to the back room where the family spent most of their time; it was a mark of prosperity that the 'front room' was used only for special occasions.[23]

By the 1890s, many of those who promoted public health had shifted their focus to the insides of houses and the habits of the people. Tuberculosis became more of an issue, not because its death toll had increased, but because mortality from other diseases was falling faster. The popularising of 'germ theory' in the 1880s made TB into an infectious disease – no longer just a common way of wasting away. There was now a germ for TB, and people could be tested. That fact, however, did not transform common practices because it was soon discovered that almost everyone had been infected at some time. The question then became, under what conditions did TB germs make you ill, and the answers concerned ventilation, overcrowding and nutrition.[24] These were the factors investigated in Manchester and Salford by a new generation of public health doctors and other medics, including J. F. W. Tatham, the young MOH for Salford and a skilled statistician who went on to join the office of the Registrar General; Arthur Ransome, a local GP who took a particular interest in TB and was for decades the major prop of the MSSA; and James Niven, who was to be MOH of Manchester for about thirty years.

At the University medical school, the Swiss pathologist Sheridan Delépine specialised in bacteriology and set up one of the first public health laboratories. Other 'scientific clinicians' also contributed to public health issues, including William Japp Sinclair, the obstetrician who popularised the story of Ignaz Semmelweis' unsuccessful advocacy of cleanliness to avoid child-bed fever; Sinclair himself was an expert on venereal disease (VD).[25]

From 1889, the Victoria University granted a Diploma in Sanitary Science to medical practitioners who had attended special laboratory courses in the Pathological and Chemical Departments. Aware that recent advances in the knowledge of bacteriology could provide great assistance to the local sanitary authorities, Delépine successfully petitioned the University to establish one of the country's first Public Health Laboratories Service. He worked closely with Niven, advising on the correct use of steam as a disinfectant, and on house flies and their role in the spread of summer diarrhoea.[26]

Key figures in
public health in
nineteenth-century
Manchester:
(a) James Phillips
Kay-Shuttleworth;
(b) Edwin
Chadwick;
(c) Dr John Leigh;
(d) Dr John Tatham;
(e) Prof.
A. S. Delépine;
(f) Dr James Niven.

a

b

c

d

e

f

The consciousness of germs also became part of the campaign against infant mortality. It was a central element in efforts to educate mothers, who doctors and reformers now considered to require hygienic knowledge to supplement or replace their traditional mothering skills. Flies, previously regarded by rich and poor alike as no more than a nuisance, became the carriers of germs – the 'home' equivalent of the tropical mosquitoes, newly revealed as the agents of malaria. And if the flies were full of germs, it was probably because they had visited some unguarded privy. Thus the old theme that dirt caused disease became particularised by the latest science.

Cleanliness was crucial if babies were to be saved and raised for the nation. So too was medical surveillance. By the Edwardian period, school children would have periodic medical inspections and some provision for special hospital services, e.g. for the removal of tonsils. They might well receive school dinners, and some would go on summer holidays, usually to North Wales, courtesy of a children's charity or lad's club.

It was to these voluntary and municipal initiatives that Manchester's improvers pointed when quizzed about the extraordinary proportion of Manchester youths who volunteered for service in the Boer War and were turned down as unfit. This statistic became notorious evidence for claims that the race was degenerating. It helped create support for 'eugenics' or the practice of better breeding, because some people were now despairing of environmental improvements and putting their faith in the new science of genetics. Their interest in eugenics, usually amounted to a belief that the middle classes should breed more and the poor should breed less, so as not to transmit the weak constitutions which predisposed them to tuberculosis, alcoholism, prostitution, and crime. The handicapped, and especially the feeble-minded, were not to breed at all: they were to live in colonies where they would be protected from exploitation as well as reproduction.[27] (Colonies were then topical; an epileptic colony at Langho in the Ribble valley was developed by Manchester Poor Law Guardians,[28] and there were also colonies for TB.) Eugenic views were widely shared, but not by the majority of MOsH, nor by the majority of Manchester sanitarians, for whom the statistics pointed to gradual improvement since the mid century. For them it was clear that each generation enjoyed an advantage over their parents, a secular betterment which they attributed to environmental improvements. To the working classes, improvement often seemed to depend on higher wages and the chance to move to better housing and eat better food.

In the agencies for improvement around 1900, one sees the symbiosis of charitable and statutory activity, for example in the medical services for sick children. They were identified by school doctors and sent to school clinics, or perhaps to the local charity hospitals which were removing large numbers of tonsils, for which they came to be subsidised by the local authorities. For the old, the main benefit was state pensions, which gave a choice other than work or workhouse. For working men, and for those women who worked outside the home, it was access to general practitioners through a state insurance system where workers' contributions were matched with employer and government payments.[29]

It is perhaps in connection with maternity that one sees most fully the synergies of local philanthropy, medical initiatives, and national legislation that were so characteristic of late Victorian and Edwardian Britain. From 1890, the City Council paid for some of the working-class visitors who had been employed by the LSA. And as worries about the size and strength of the population increased around 1900, a series of statutory means were implemented as local initiatives or under national pressure – hence the supply of municipal midwives, of schools for mothers, and of more accommodation in maternity hospitals.[30]

Much of the agitation and social experimentation was local: successful measures could then be generalised through the networks of philanthropy, or of 'social science', or MOsH; some of them would then be supported or prescribed through national legislation. That developmental pattern was to weaken between the wars, as local economies crashed and national state power increased.

Between the Wars

If the period from 1890 to 1914 saw rapid development of sanitation and welfare measures, the interwar years saw a consolidation and expansion of municipal responsibilities. If the pre-war decades had been politically and economically turbulent, the 1920s would see a rapid decline in the textile industry and coal mining – both hitting Lancashire hard. Slowly it became clear that the old industrial order, disrupted by the Great War, would not be re-established. Before the war, Manchester had been the global capital of the cotton industry; it would become a city of mixed industrial fortune in a region that was economically depressed until the Second World War.

Nationally, the depression of the early 1920s long postponed the wartime hopes of building 'homes fit for heroes.' But a Ministry of Health was established to cover poor law and public health responsibilities, and local authorities were given more powers, including new provisions for tuberculosis which was then seen as a major problem for working men and hence the industrial economy (see

Figure 2.3 Death rate (per 1000 persons) from respiratory tuberculosis in Manchester, 1900–1940.

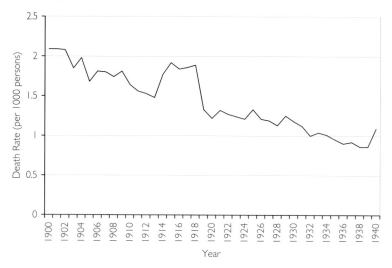

Source: Manchester MOH Reports, 1901–1940.

figure 2.3).[31] Both Manchester City and Lancashire County councils built sanatoria and surgical hospitals, as well as clinics and domiciliary services. There were also 'special clinics' for VD, a major wartime problem.

Where pre-war reformers had focussed on infants, the interwar decades extended their concern to include maternal health, creating ante-natal clinics and more maternity homes. The supporters of these initiatives were often women who had fought successfully for the vote and then taken up additional women's issues. Better education and facilities made a difference. Infants and children still caught most of the usual infections and might be taken to the infectious disease hospital, but as standards of nutrition and nursing care improved, the children were less likely to die. Against the threat of diphtheria there was now a vaccine, which Manchester's public health doctors worked hard to popularise. It helped too, that some of the worst slums were cleared.

Where the 1890s had seen the first social housing, and the 1900s new model suburbs, both public and private, the interwar decades saw large housing estates designed to replace some of the worst of the Victorian housing stock. Manchester's largest, at Wythenshawe, was the creation of Ernest and Sheena Simon, who were both members of the city council, first as Liberals and then for Labour. He was the son of an immigrant engineer from Germany, who built a successful business; she was a relation of Beatrice Potter, who with her husband Sydney Webb led the Fabians in their fight for 'scientific socialism'.[32] Wythenshawe was expected to be more than a huge estate in a southern extension of the city; it was meant as a satellite town with its own centre and industries. However, the latter barely materialised and many of the new inhabitants had to commute to jobs in 'Trafford Park' developed alongside the ship canal from about 1900 and the English home of several key American companies. The decades around the Second World War were a hopeful time for many of Manchester's poorer citizens, moved from slums to new estates with electricity in their homes and lots of green spaces between. Re-housing came under the public health department which grew rapidly as new responsibilities were added to the council's agenda.

The MOH from 1894 to 1922 was James Niven, as noted, followed by Veitch Clark; both were Scots, like so many MOsH. Niven had focussed on infectious diseases and especially TB; Veitch Clark saw a major increase in powers when the Poor Law was finally ended after 1929, and the workhouses and associated hospitals were transferred to municipalities and county councils. Manchester City Council took over Crumpsall and Withington: the workhouses were to be run by the Public Assistance Committee, the hospital sections were transferred to the Public Health Committee, along with Booth Hall, which had been developed as a hospital for poor children. Since the

Aerial View
of Benchill
Housing Estate,
Wythenshawe,
Manchester, 1937.

© MANCHESTER
LIBRARIES.

MOH already supervised Monsall, this amounted to a formidable responsibility (c. 2500 beds).

In developing the municipal hospital services, Veitch Clark and his staff worked closely with the medical school and the consultants attached to the Royal Infirmary. Indeed, Manchester became a national model for co-operation between municipal and charity hospitals, in stark contrast to the bitter relationships between the two sectors in London. In some ways, Manchester pointed the way for national reformers, then scheming for a more ordered system of hospitals. During the Second World War, hospital co-ordination and re-development became a major theme in the intense professional and public discussions about the post-war world which would follow victory. Most observers, and the Ministry of Health, expected that the local authorities would continue to extend their remits; but many doctors and supporters of charities feared that outcome.

In fact, as we shall see, under the Labour Government of 1945 all the hospitals were nationalised and run by regional boards and local committees which were chosen by the government, not by the municipalities. The elite of the Manchester Medical School, already prominent in hospital planning, came to dominate the early years of the NHS in this region. By contrast, the City Council, which in 1943 had expected to run primary care and expand its hospitals, found its health responsibilities reduced to sanitation and clinics – much as in 1914.

Postscript

This chapter on the early history of public health issues and services in Manchester provides the background canvas for the vast changes that were to come after the Second World War. It presents a cumulation of concerns, from fever nests to districts of high mortality; from houses and infrastructure to the control of specific infections; and from the promotion of the population's health, especially through better motherhood, to disease prevention by vaccines.

After the Second World War, none of these general concerns became irrelevant. But the older fears of filthy districts and of specific infections seemed to fade, so too did the apparent need for a large and healthy national population, ready to work, fight or populate the empire. Medicine seemed to be entering a new world where infections and poverty were more or less conquered and chronic disease was the emergent problem. How then, under and around the new NHS, would the proponents of public health services defend old gains and take on new challenges?

Post-war Public Health: From the Introduction of the NHS to its Re-organisation in 1974

T HE GREAT WAR, medically speaking, had been improvised, but the Second World War was planned. By 1945 public medicine seemed to epitomise successful national organisation. The Emergency Hospital Service had taken over the running of hospitals and arranged for the treatment of bomb casualties; the rationing of food and the supply of vitamins, etc., had ensured that civilian health was rather better than in peace time (excepting the TB and other patients who were turned out of their sanatoria to make space for war casualties); and penicillin was an icon of war-time research.[1]

Whereas the hopes of peace and prosperity after the Great War had soon been threatened and dashed, those who planned the future in the Second World War were determined that their schemes for a comprehensive welfare state would be fulfilled. Popular attachment to that vision was a major reason for the unexpected defeat of Churchill in the 1945 election and the creation of the first secure Labour Party government. Its initial achievements were considerable, including the extension of secondary education and the better support of universities and science. Its nationalisation plans included private industries such as coal and steel, as well as utilities largely developed by city governments, such as gas, water and electricity. Amongst the most popular of the reforms was the National Health Service, discussed throughout the war but radically redesigned by Aneurin Bevan when he was made Minister of Health in the Attlee government.[2]

By nationalising all hospitals, both charity and tax-supported, Bevan cut through the long arguments about how the two kinds of hospitals could be related, and how that complex system could best be planned. He initially suggested that public health functions would be included in the same national structure, but soon saw that inclusion as impractical. Such a move would also have been a further blow to the (mostly Labour) councils whose dreams of expanding municipal health services were being dismantled by a Labour minister. So, for convenience and to restrict controversy, public health functions were left with the municipal and county councils. And to quieten the general practitioners who were opposing the NHS plans, primary care went largely unreformed, except that the whole population, not just those employed outside the home, would have access to healthcare free at the point of delivery.

This tripartite division, of hospitals, public health, and general practice was, perhaps inevitable given the antagonism of most doctors to local authority control, but it was unfortunate in many ways. It fragmented the municipal services for TB and maternity, which had been notable for the range of co-ordinated functions, from domiciliary services to special hospitals. It maintained the isolation of GPs, who some reformers were trying to tempt into health centres alongside public health workers. The division also underlined the dominance and apparent importance of hospitals, a view which had increased in power through the interwar decades as hospital medicine had become more technical and expensive, and as transferred Poor-Law hospitals had become the leading edge of municipal services. Public health doctors and some of their socialist supporters might argue clinical medicine was less important to overall health than good diets and cleanliness, but these simple preventives had little cachet in an age that was hugely impressed with the miracles of science. Indeed, it seemed to some reformist doctors that if antibiotics could cure infections, and if the new welfare state could greatly diminish poverty and malnutrition, then the medicine of the future would be about treatments for chronic disease, such as cancer and cardio-vascular disease, and genetic conditions. The way forward, as in cancer, would be earlier or more radical treatments, including surgery and new ranges of drugs. In this vision, traditional public health measures were easily marginalised, and GPs tended to be seen as little more than gatekeepers for hospitals.

This vision also drew away from the localism and community involvement which had been so characteristic of the British tradition since the middle of the nineteenth century. During the Second World War some advocates of local government had argued that health services needed to be locally run, not just to meet local needs, but because they were among the most interesting aspects of local politics. As long as water came out of the taps, few people cared whether the utility was municipal or national – private utilities had long ago been discredited – but health services engaged people. Without that engagement, public interest in local politics would decline, and men and women would no longer get the training and experience which might lead to local leadership and national office. Critics were right, but bound to lose; and the role and influence of local government did decline.

In 1945, Manchester council had provided gas, water, electricity and hospitals, but nationalisation removed these powers, leaving transport, houses, clinics, old people's homes and domiciliary services. In the interwar decades, local authorities had become more dependent on national subsidies, and less on their own direct revenues, partly to protect the industrially depressed districts by transfer of monies from the more prosperous south. After the Second World War this problem remained, even as the municipal functions diminished. By the end of the twentieth century, municipalities were effectively reduced to local agencies of national programmes.

One might argue that the move from voluntarism to statutory services (e.g. for hospitals), and from local to national control also undermined local charities and community involvement. This is an important argument, with continuing ramifications for public health, but it is only part of the story.[3] Robert Putnam has claimed for the USA, that the post Second World War decades saw rapid declines in the membership and activity of the many and diverse voluntary groups which had grown from the later nineteenth century as means of socialising the young and securing local cohesion. From the Boy Scouts to Women's Institutes, from local drama groups to sports clubs, public participation declined. And for Britain, more than the US, one might include the continued decline of organised religion, whose churches and chapels had provided contexts for many social activities and educational groups. Later, one could note the decline of trade unions, and the local political clubs which often became little more than drinking venues.[4]

But there were also contrary movements, with new forms of sociability and politics. Examples related to public health include wider public involvement in disease oriented charities, e.g. for cancer, or in 'non-governmental' international agencies, such as Oxfam or Save the Children, or in new single issue campaign, such as CND or Greenpeace. Importantly, the rise of a new feminism from the 1960s in some ways offset the decline of older groups, such as the Women's Institutes or the Co-operative Women's Guild, which had spread public health messages and pushed for better maternity facilities. Though most of these new agencies were not focussed on the welfare of particular localities, the 1960s also saw new kinds of community representation, which in the 1970s also extended into the NHS.

These shifts in the structure and attitudes of British society changed the social and geographical contexts of public health efforts. New industrial organisation meant that local ownership of large businesses became rare; scholarships meant that fewer bright children stayed in their native communities; and generally the workforce became more mobile. Especially from the 1960s onward, more married women went out to work, so less of their time was available to provide voluntary labour to community groups. Then there was 'the telly' and the changes in leisure patterns it exemplified. Especially after the coronation of 1953, staying at home became more attractive. And when the telly faded as a public focus after the 1970s, there were computers and the internet at home. When one had the time and money to go out, there was ever more shopping, restaurants and drinking.

After the Second World War, in an age of atomic weapons and promises of automation, decolonisation and immigration, the early twentieth-century concern with the health and size of the native population slipped quietly away. Britain no longer needed big armies or massed labour, and if particular kinds of workers were required, they could be imported. So too, in an age of increased social mobility and home entertainment, the expectation of community involvement faded. But these changes were slow, as we can see in the local medical services, where nationalisation initially served to extend the power of certain technical and social elites who were strongly embedded in Manchester and its region.

The New NHS and Public Health

The National Health Service came into operation on 5 July 1948. On that 'appointed day', all the municipal and charity hospitals were nationalised. In future they would be run by regional boards and local committees chosen by the government, much to the resentment of city councils who had anticipated extending their control of institutional care.

Contrary to much recent propaganda, the early NHS was far from being a Soviet-style monolith. Many local philanthropists were appointed to Regional Boards and to Hospital Management Committees, and most hospitals maintained their 'friends' groups and volunteers, though these were now supplementary rather than vital. The leaders of the NHS in the Manchester region were mostly key figures in the medical school. Some, like Robert Platt, the full-time Professor of Medicine, had moved here after the war and went on to attain national eminence; but several others had a long history of local (and national) service. Sir John (later Lord) Stopford, the first chair of the Manchester Regional Hospital Board (MRHB), was concurrently the head of Manchester University. As a medically qualified anatomist, he had helped lead the medical school through the twenties and thirties; he had played a key role in local hospital planning, and in wartime plans for the reform of British medical education. One of his former students became the first Senior Administrative Medical Officer of the MRHB, whilst two of his close friends from student days helped shape specialist services in and beyond the Manchester region: Sir Harry Platt was a national leader in orthopaedics, Sir Geoffrey Jefferson in neurosurgery.[5]

The salaries which hospital consultants and academics now received from the NHS, gave them more time for research and developing services. Notable local examples, supported by the regional NHS more than by national research funds, include John Charnley's orthopaedic work at Wrightington, near Wigan, that provided the international model for joint replacement;[6] and the world's first test tube baby, a result of painstaking (and professionally unpopular) research on laparoscopy by Patrick Steptoe at Oldham. Within the NHS hospitals there were new freedoms, and through the 1960s there remained much scope for local service initiatives, including the pioneering general-hospital psychiatry units developed in the former cotton towns around Manchester.[7]

Losing their municipal hospitals certainly dealt a heavy blow to the MOsH, and some historians have argued that many then showed a lack of imagination that hastened the demise of local authority public health.[8] MOsH stand accused of not adjusting to advances in social work, or the decline of infectious diseases, or shifts in general practice; they were slow to develop new services in community care and health education. But more recent historical research has come to their defence, suggesting that some MOsH were commendably innovative, albeit in difficult circumstances.[9] As a medical specialism, public health was undoubtedly overshadowed by the technical advances in acute care, which received the lion's share of public funding and media attention. And in Manchester, as elsewhere in Britain, post-war austerity delayed the realisation of public health schemes.

In accordance with Part III of the NHS Act (1946), Local Authorities were left accountable for health services based in the community, specifically the care of mothers and young children, midwifery, health visiting, home nursing, domestic help, vaccination and immunisation, ambulances, the prevention of illness, care and after-care, mental health, and health education. They also remained responsible for sanitation.

We shall see that Metcalfe Brown, the Manchester MOH from 1942 to 1967, emphasised environmental health and family welfare, and made some progress in community care and health education, in spite of shortages. Meanwhile, the post-war University excelled at thinking about health in broader terms and developing services. Only at the end of the 1960s did the outlook for public health in Manchester turn sour. The national recognition of social work as an independent profession, and the creation of social services departments separate from public health, deprived a new MOH, Kennedy Campbell, of another slice of the former health responsibilities. Though the remaining services continued to improve by degrees, an NHS re-organisation was looming, and resignation and complacency seem to have set in, with little incentive to promote new areas of work beyond the statutory requirements. In 1974, local public health departments were abolished, as was the post of MOH.

Charles Metcalfe Brown and Local Authority Health Services, 1948–1967

Manchester's MOH, Charles Metcalfe Brown, hailed the NHS as 'a landmark in the history of public health legislation.' 'Time may prove it to be', he continued, 'the most important and far-reaching Act of Parliament, as regards health measures, passed since the first Public Health Act of 1848'.[10] In a paper delivered in October that year, Metcalfe Brown urged his fellow professionals to 'look forward rather than back', and to consider the potential for development in child health services, the building of health centres, industrial medicine, the care of the aged, mass-immunisation programmes, smoke abatement, the social and psychological causes of ill health, the compiling of medical statistics, health education, and teaching.[11] In his 1948 report on the health of the city, he praised the introduction of the NHS for raising the status of preventive medicine. 'Preventive medicine', he wrote, 'is vastly more important than therapeutic medicine – as the first improves in efficiency and results, so must the other diminish'.[12] As despondency among MOsH persisted into the following decade, Metcalfe Brown was resilient in his optimism. As President of the Society of Medical Officers of Health in 1953, he reminded his colleagues that theirs was 'the only true health service at present'.[13] With hospitals and general practice dealing almost exclusively with the sick and the injured, the title of 'National Health Service' was, he argued, a misnomer.

As required by Part III of the NHS Act, the Manchester department set about expanding its existing community-based services and developing new ones. Some services were amalgamated: for example, home helps and domestic helps now formed a single Domestic Helps service. Other services previously delivered by a number of different agencies were placed under the direct administrative control of the Health Committee, as in the case of home nursing and the Manchester ambulance services, although close liaison with external agencies remained crucial. (See appendix 2a.)

Public health now also included mental health, at least in its 'community' aspects, and a City of Manchester Mental Health Service was set up in 1948. The NHS Act had abolished the Lancashire Mental Hospitals Board and the Mental Deficiency Acts Committee, an unwieldy federation of local authorities which since the late nineteenth century had run all the major asylums within the geographical county. The control of the asylums had passed to Regional Hospital Boards; the local authorities only got the clinics and the social workers. The asylums, however, rarely became linked with local general hospitals. Each of the huge institutions, including Prestwich Asylum (just north of Manchester), were assigned their own Hospital Management Committees and continued in their accustomed isolation.

For most of its mental health services, Manchester was a 'follower' when other nearby authorities were setting the pace. In Salford, a particularly imaginative MOH, J. Lancelot Burn, collaborated with Manchester University in developing community medical services, intended to keep sufferers out of hospitals, and incorporating one of the first computerised patient registers.[14] In Oldham, the Manchester Regional Board experimented with the appointment of a consultant psychiatrist to a district general hospital. Arthur Pool had been superintendent of the famous York Retreat, and he soon established a collaboration with the Oldham MOH; together they developed day centres and workshops which foreshadowed later developments in 'community care'.[15] Progress in Manchester itself was more conventional, but by the 1960s, mental health provision had expanded enough to warrant its own division. By then, Manchester City Council was providing mental health training centres, day centres and clubs, and across the country, asylums were becoming more integrated with local hospitals, as well as with local authority services. But asylums were hard to staff and expensive to maintain. They seemed less necessary as tranquilisers were introduced, and after the 1962 national Hospital Plan, were expected to run down. The future of psychiatric services in Britain, as already in Lancashire, was to lie largely with district general hospitals and 'community services'.

For NHS and Local Authority health services, however, developments often depended on the construction of new buildings, and they were often delayed by a shortage of technical staff and the conflicting demands of other capital projects. For the allocation of resources, Metcalfe Brown saw the city's poor and insufficient housing

Figure 3.1   Trends in infant mortality in Manchester, 1945–1971.

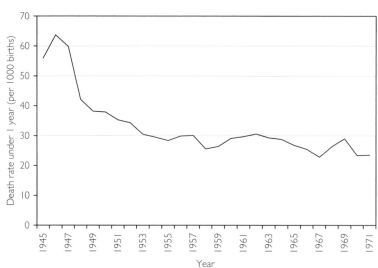

Source: Manchester MOH Reports, 1945–1971.

stock as 'the greatest and most urgent public health problem'.[16] Slum clearances had been postponed during the war and only resumed piecemeal in 1951.

As shown in figure 3.1, the decline in infant mortality slowed down after the Second World War, and rates of infant deaths actually rose for five consecutive years between 1957 and 1962. This state of affairs was blamed on a shortage of ante-natal and maternity beds in hospitals, and on the damp and defective dwellings in which new babies were living and dying. In 1957, Manchester needed 83,000 houses, of which 62,000 were to replace unfit dwellings.[17] At the then current rate, clearing the slums would take up to forty years. The Health Department was frustrated by the failure of the City to provide sufficient land.

Where services were less dependent on bricks and mortar, Metcalfe Brown succeeded in pushing for change, sometimes assisted by the powers invested by the Manchester Corporation Act, 1946, which permitted the creation of services independent of statutory legislation, upon the approval of the Ministry of Health. An amendment to the Act in 1954, gave Manchester the power to conduct research into new public health schemes, including smoke prevention and cervical cytology.

Smoke abatement, as opposed to prevention, had been a statutory duty of local authorities since 1926. Manchester, in 1924, had led the way through the formation of the Manchester Regional Joint Smoke Abatement Committee, covering a fifteen mile radius from the city centre. The sharp increase in the death rate during the 'London fog' at the end of 1952, renewed concern about the problems of smoke, and in Salford, J. Lancelot Burn was already pressing for smoke-free zones. (He once suggested that Salfordians with breathing problems might seek refuge from smog by wearing their war-issue gas masks inside air-conditioned cinemas.)[18] The Manchester central smokeless zone, extending over 104 acres of the city centre, was established on 1 May 1952, three years before the government introduced its own Clean Air Bill. It proved surprisingly effective, and featured in a BBC TV programme in 1953.[19] Over the next decade, Manchester continued to promote smoke prevention, holding a national industrial-fuel efficiency exhibition in 1955, the largest exhibition of its type to be held in the provinces, and providing financial incentives to those trained in the correct use of industrial boilers and furnaces. By 1966, thirty-five per cent of premises in Manchester were subject to smokeless zone or smoke control orders.

Two decades after the introduction of Clean Air legislation and smokeless zones, the skies over Manchester, as in other large towns and cities, began to clear. This had a noticeable effect on health.[20] The death rate from bronchitis declined (see figure 3.2). While general factors such as improved nutrition, better medicine, and better working and living environments surely had an impact, the reduction in atmospheric pollution almost certainly contributed to the overall improvement in chronic respiratory conditions.[21]

Figure 3.2 Death rate (per 1000 population) from bronchitis in Manchester, 1901–1975.

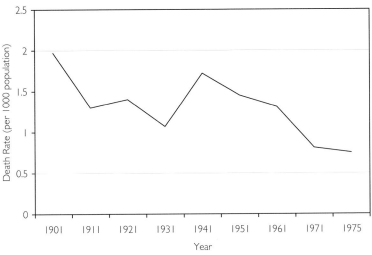

Source: Manchester Environmental Health Department Annual Report, 1976.

Manchester Town
Hall during cleaning
1967.

The success of smoke prevention also enabled over eighty years of
air pollution to be cleared from the stonework of Manchester's civic
buildings. Soon the natural colours of stone and brick emerged in
a city centre which had been black. Paradoxically, one of the major
contestations about smokeless fuel concerned the new hospital the
MRHB had planned for Wythenshawe. The City Council wanted it
smokeless, but the MRHB wanted to avoid additional expense.

MOsH have sometimes been accused of continuing the early
twentieth-century focus on mothers, infants and children, but not
addressing the needs of adolescents and 'problem families', yet
Metcalfe Brown repeatedly noted how the health visitor's casework
was extending to cover the whole family, and how teamwork among

professionals would build a healthy society founded on 'happy family units'.[22] In 1948, he supported the establishment of the Manchester Family Welfare Service, the brainchild of Lady Gertrude Jefferson (the wife of the neurosurgeon, Sir Geoffrey Jefferson), a trained psychiatrist and former medical officer in maternity and child welfare, who focussed on the emotional and psychological problems of children and their parents. As a 'preventive and constructive service', the Family Welfare Service aimed at 'stabilising family life by preventing, if possible in the early stages, wrong tendencies which if allowed to continue are likely to lead to nervous breakdown, broken marriages, delinquency and much general unhappiness, especially where there are children.'[23] The service followed a broader trend in the reconstruction of post-war British society, a growing culture of consultation and conciliation in public and private life, also reflected in the establishment of the National Marriage Guidance Council.

By 1966, the Family Welfare Service had dealt with more than 4,500 attendances, had established four centres across the city, and had become a recognised branch of the Public Health Service. It worked closely with the Maternity and Child Welfare Centres, often sharing premises and staff, and the service received referrals from GPs, health visitors and other social work agencies, including probation officers, almoners and the clergy. The service was used as a model by other health authorities, including Bristol, and Salford (in 1952).[24]

In 'community care', the Health Department's record was less than satisfactory, but again some progress was made. After much delay, new mental health institutions, including junior and adult training and residential units, day centres and clubs, and hostels were finally built from the mid 1960s onwards. The domiciliary care of the aged and infirm was also extended, imposing an ever heavier burden on the department. The number of aged and infirm persons dealt with by health visitors rose from fourteen in 1948, to 1,872 in 1957, and the number of visits from 123 to 7,488.[25] While the National Assistance Act (1948) allowed for the compulsory removal of the elderly to hospitals or welfare homes, the Health Department was gratified that the number of compulsory removals fell from twenty-six in 1956 to just one in 1966.[26] The domiciliary services were considered crucial to avoiding compulsory removal.[27] Persuasion, tact and patience were considered the 'key-notes' of the service, intended to 'minimise the numerous fears and suspicions that old people easily develop'.[28]

In 1964, the Health Department took over the direct operation of a chiropody service for priority groups such as the elderly, the physically disabled, and expectant mothers. Until that point, the service had been run by voluntary organisations with only financial support from the Health Committee. The Home Help Service also expanded to meet the increase in necessitous cases, and was particularly praised for providing the 'most valuable regular aid for elderly and infirm persons'.[29] Yet in 1966, Metcalfe Brown was drawn to comment that 'the average amount of help which can be given to elderly people is still, in my view, too low'.[30]

The Health Department was also keen to take on health education, trying to promote healthy habits, the right attitudes of mind, and knowledge of the correct way of living.[31] Even before the NHS, Metcalfe Brown had encouraged his fellow health officers to harness the 'modern methods of publicity' – newsprint, radio, loud speaker, public transport advertisement, and film, for the purposes of health education.[32] From 1948, he did just that. Manchester Health Department appointed staff, held lectures, exhibitions and classes, and distributed leaflets, magazines, posters and films. They maintained contact with a variety of outside bodies, including the Central Council for Health Education, the National Film Library, and the National Association for the Prevention of Tuberculosis, and they encouraged media reporting of their work (as for the smoke prevention scheme). A 'Heath of the People Exhibition' held over two weeks in 1948 in the demonstration hall of the Gas Department, was publicised by the BBC and the local press; it attracted five to six thousand people including 600 school children.

Targeted health education campaigns included diphtheria immunisation, the prevention of accidents in the home, and cancer. Manchester was an early adapter of cancer research, education and screening programmes. The Manchester Committee on Cancer (MCC) had conducted fundraising and publicity for cancer research in the northwest since the 1920s. It consisted of lay and professional representatives from the Health Committee, the University, the Royal Infirmary, the Christie Hospital, the Holt Radium Institute, and the other large Manchester hospitals. Its aims were to create a unified and integrated approach to cancer research. An early investigation, supported by MOH Veitch Clark, had been to determine the cause of carcinogenic properties of the mineral oils used in the lubrication of spinning mules in Lancashire cotton mills, which was producing an incidence of cancer of the skin of the scrotum thirty times greater than that of the rest of the population of the country. The introduction of 'safer' lubricating oils, and minimising bodily contact with them, significantly reduced the incidence of mule spinners' cancer.[33]

In the 1950s, the MCC began investigating lay understandings of cancer, with the aim of tackling delays in seeking medical attention for breast and cervical cancer. Through surveys of Manchester women, and detailed interviews with cancer patients, their families and doctors, the MCC experiment revealed that the challenge for cancer control was not so much the public's ignorance of the disease's symptoms, as was often assumed, but rather a fear of the consequences of cancer that derived from personal experience, including the associated pain and incurability. A unique educational programme was devised, based on local newspaper articles and meetings with local community groups, where stories of cancer treatment were told through the voices of former sufferers. Though change in public opinion was gradual, the Manchester campaign was deemed a success by its leaders. Lay cancer education was re-oriented away from propaganda based on fear, and towards that which stressed the more hopeful aspects of early treatment. The approach achieved national prominence, and members of the education group were frequently consulted by the Ministry of Health.[34]

Manchester's Christie Hospital was central to Manchester's cancer efforts. Prominent figures on the MCC education group included Ralston Paterson, the radiotherapist director of the Christie Hospital and Holt Radium Institute, and John Wakefield, the MCC's executive officer, and later, Director of the Department of Social Research, also based at the Christie and Holt Radium Institute. The Christie piloted Manchester's first cytological screening programme in the early 1960s, to examine both the problems of screening symptomless women, and the effectiveness of screening women of all ages. Research to uncover trends in screening, the survey of attitudes and action, and public education were again important elements of the cytology programme.[35] The Manchester Health Department was invited to participate in the scheme, and in October 1963, pending approval by the Ministry of Health, introduced screening clinics as a research project under the powers granted in the Manchester Corporation Act, 1954.[36]

Later, the Health Department also collaborated with the MCC in promoting the link between smoking and lung cancer, leading the distribution and display of posters showing the positive link between cigarettes and the disease. On this issue, it was Manchester's medical experts who were once again prominent on the national scene. It was Robert Platt, the first full-time Professor of Medicine at the University of Manchester (1945–1965), who, as President of the Royal College of Physicians (1957–1962), had led the publication of the first College report on Smoking and Health in 1962. As a city, Manchester was a beacon in terms of cancer research in this period. The MCC was regularly consulted over the production of television documentaries on cancer. In January 1966, the city featured heavily in the BBC's Panorama programme dedicated to

Figure 3.3   Death rate (per 1000 persons) from all causes, Manchester Local Authority, 1945–1973.

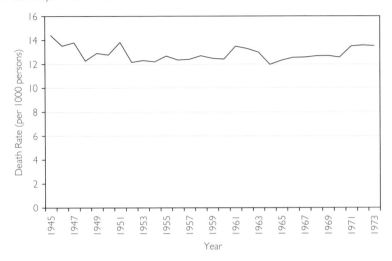

Source: Manchester MOH Reports, 1945–1973.

Figure 3.4   Death rates (per 1000 persons) from all causes, Manchester, Salford, Liverpool, Birmingham, and Glasgow Local Authorities, 1945–1972.

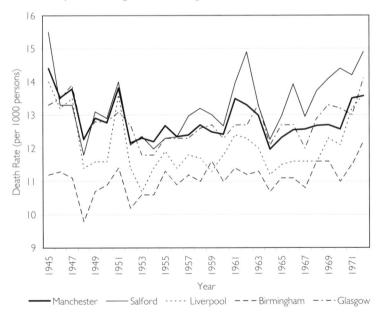

Source: Manchester, Salford, Birmingham, Liverpool and Glasgow MOH Reports, 1945–1972.

the memory of the late Richard Dimbleby, who had died of cancer the previous year. The broadcast attracted 'keen local interest and a national audience'.[37]

In the early 1960s, Manchester experienced a rise in death rates which can probably be attributed to the sharp rise in infant mortality referred to previously, and a slight increase in deaths from TB, lung cancer, and bronchitis (see figure 3.3). Manchester also compared badly alongside other major cities, with the exception perhaps of neighbouring Salford (see figure 3.4).

Despite the persistent health problems, Metcalfe Brown remained optimistic, but he recognised the disadvantages to health inherent in a commercial and industrial city such as Manchester, with its unfavourable climate and bad housing. Nor did he disguise the limitations or failures of the city's public health services. He retired in the mid sixties, when the contraceptive pill was coming into general use, arguing that the increasing incidence of venereal disease would require serious and sustained national and local health education.

The Manchester School of Public Health and the Development of Social Medicine

Shortly after the Second World War, public health was taken out of the University department of bacteriology, in the hope that a separate department of preventive medicine and public health could better meet the changing demands of postgraduate and undergraduate education under the health service. As we shall see, the move also reflected John Stopford's interest in the discipline of Social Medicine, then being promoted nationally by Professor John Ryle. The aim was to interest clinicians in the social context of diseases; public health would no longer be just for local authorities, MOsH, and bacteriologists. This orientation matched Stopford's own deep involvement with the NHS, his promotion of research and teaching in industrial diseases, especially rheumatism, and Manchester's experiments in the teaching of general practice.

The Diploma in Public Health (DPH) syllabus was revised in 1945 to include a dissertation, and to differentiate between practitioners requiring legal recognition as MOsH, and those who intended to engage in other kinds of work related to public health.[38] With its new focus on preventive medicine, the department distanced itself from lectures on hygiene, which Stopford now considered 'more suitable for plumbers and Sanitary Inspectors than medical students'.[39]

In selecting its first Professor of Preventive Medicine and Public Health, the University looked for someone with a breadth of outlook on public health. The then Professor of Bacteriology and Preventive Medicine, and Director of the Public Health Laboratories, H. B. Maitland, preferred to appoint an epidemiologist, who being neither strictly an administrator nor strictly a clinician, might ensure a smooth integration of the new department within the Medical School. In 1947 they appointed Dr Andrew Topping, who since 1944 had been Director of Health Division, and Deputy Chief of Relief Services, at the United Nations Relief and Rehabilitation Administration.

When informally accepting the appointment, Topping wrote to the Vice-Chancellor of his 'sad lack of scientific knowledge'; but, it seems, his practical experience more than compensated. He had been assistant county MOH for Lancashire (1925–30), then MOH for Rochdale (1930–32), and finally a senior Medical Officer for London County Council (1932–1940). It was in Rochdale that Topping had made his reputation, by securing a dramatic reduction in rates of maternal mortality which had been the highest in the country. Many local medical practitioners had blamed malnutrition and the employment of women in the mills, but by re-investigating the deaths, Topping uncovered poor antenatal care, with evidence of unnecessary and often violent interference, and of shock and haemorrhage following difficult labours. He launched a publicity campaign, using lectures, press reports and health visitors to enlighten the public to the 'true facts' of maternal mortality. Pregnant women, midwives, doctors and consultants were informed about antenatal care, about adequate preparation for confinement, and the dangers of inducing labour.[40] Between his Rochdale years and Manchester, Topping had worked on smallpox, hospital administration and European health problems, with five years as a Lecturer in Public Health at Charing Cross Hospital Medical School in London.

The new professor was expected to embrace 'Social Medicine', stressing the broader determinants of ill health, including poverty and the environment, and the need for political action to change these conditions – as organisations such as the Socialist Medical Association had maintained through the 1930s. During the war, this new field had developed fast, furthered by Oxford University's appointment of John Ryle to the first Chair of Social Medicine in 1942. In 1943, the Interim Report of the Royal College of Physicians of London had recommended that every medical school establish a department of social and preventive medicine, and integrate the subject into clinical studies. The same thrust was repeated in the government's programme for medical education, prescribed in 1944 by the Goodenough Committee, of which Stopford was deputy chairman. Key chairs in Social Medicine were given to F. A. E. Crew at Edinburgh in 1944, and Thomas McKeown at Birmingham in 1945; the UK Society of Social Medicine followed in 1956.

Topping recognised the value of combining the clinical and social aspects of medical education, believing that the 'doctor who is not fully cognisant of the part played by avoidable factors in lessening health, mental and bodily, is not competent to pull his full weight as a family doctor or as a specialist'.[41] In a letter to Stopford in 1949, Topping expressed his hope that a 'real' social medicine department would soon develop, with industrial medicine, child health and medical statistics working in co-operation.[42] In 1950, when Topping resigned to become Dean of the London School of Hygiene and Tropical Medicine (LSHTM), the Manchester chair was renamed – 'Preventive Medicine and Public Health' became 'Social and Preventive Medicine'.

The report of a sub-committee set up to explore the functions and scope of existing Chairs of Social and Preventive Medicine (April, 1950) had concluded that shifting patterns of disease would present new problems; it noted that the recently founded World Health Organisation (WHO) was demanding the promotion of physical, mental and social health, in ways which would require the co-operation of public health, clinical medicine, and social sciences. As the techniques for this type of research were as yet unknown, a man of broad education would be required in Manchester. And indeed, many of those already appointed to Chairs in Social Medicine in the UK had not come from traditional public health backgrounds: Ryle was a physician, Crew an animal geneticist, and McKeown a researcher who had investigated the effects of bombing in the Second World War. But in 1952, the University of Manchester appointed a County Medical Officer of Health to its Chair.

Colin Fraser Brockington had enjoyed a varied medical career. After qualifying, he had worked as a ship's doctor, and as Medical Officer Superintendent of the Brighton Infectious Diseases Hospital, before entering public health as Assistant County Medical Officer for Worcestershire in 1930. In 1933, he went into private practice in Devon with his GP wife, but returned to public health, first as an MOH in West Sussex (1936–1938), then as Deputy County Medical Officer for Warwickshire. In 1946, he was appointed County MOH for the West Riding of Yorkshire. Described by one colleague as a 'man of education and social concern and conscience', much of Brockington's work had focused on improving child health; in 1950 he chaired a meeting of the WHO in Geneva on School Health.[43] Through his varied experience, Brockington understood the effects of poverty and of inadequate systems of medical care.

Brockington embedded within the new department an exceptional array of individuals, including three 'inspirational' South African doctors who were also familiar with social science – Mervyn Susser, his wife Zena Stein, and Abe Adelstein who later became the

UK's Chief Medical Statistician. All three had left their homeland because of their opposition to apartheid. A fourth young doctor, the 'imaginative' Robert Logan, was supported by the Nuffield Trust for research in industrial and occupational medicine, a subject for which Manchester had appointed R. E. Lane as its first Professor.

Psychology and social anthropology were introduced to undergraduate medical training, and to the DPH course, in part it seems, because anthropology in Manchester was led by Max Gluckman, a South African and a world leader on southern Africa; and Manchester psychology had long been related to medicine. In this respect, Manchester's version of social medicine was unlike that in Birmingham, where McKeown seems to have had little time for sociologists or medical sociology.[44] In Manchester, social medicine was intellectually catholic, and junior and senior members of staff worked closely together. Brockington's other innovations included a Diploma in Community Nursing, the first pre-registration nursing education programme in a British university, and the development of the University Health Centre.

Education and Training

In the 1950s, the DPH was extended as a two-year part-time course occupying nearly 900 hours; and candidates were required to hold one or more approved posts within the Manchester region. The syllabus included public health history, law and practice; social aspects of disease; occupational health; mental health; education for health; medical statistics and social pathology; social anthropology and heredity; bacteriology and the epidemiology of infection. There was also training in social administration, one of the subjects which Manchester had helped develop, partly in connection with the NHS.[45] 'Teddy Chester,' a refugee, led an important postgraduate training programme for would-be hospital administrators, and did important research on the implementation of the NHS.[46]

While MOH for West Riding, Brockington had campaigned unsuccessfully for a revision in the training of health visitors. In an article published in the journal *Public Health* in 1949, he argued that the roles of health visitor and social worker should be combined, with all new entrants taking a university diploma course in socio-medical work.[47] The training of health visitors in hospitals, he argued, had restricted their experience of practical casework, and of the complicated structures of community; by contrast, the fieldwork training of social workers was deficient in medical or nursing experience.

At Manchester, Brockington worked hard to convince the MRHB

of the need for a revision in nursing training. (One of his leading opponents was Stopford's wife, who had been one of the first women to graduate in medicine at Manchester and was chair of the Education Committee of the Manchester Royal Infirmary.[48]) In 1953, Brockington introduced a course for nurse tutors to broaden the outlook of students and enable them to see their work in the wider context of the NHS.[49] After a long struggle against opposition from both the Manchester Royal Infirmary, and the General Nursing Council, Brockington managed in 1959 to establish the Diploma in Community Nursing as the first pre-registration, university-based course to include nursing as an academic subject. The 'Manchester Scheme', as it became known, integrated preventive and curative aspects of nursing; and alongside hospital training, it included a significant amount of community-based experience of public health. The course ran successfully for several years, and had an important influence on national policy for nurse education.[50]

Health Centres: The Future of Public Health

Health centres had been a key component of wartime plans for a new health service. Under the NHS, they retained the potential not only to renew the status of the MOH, but to also bring closer integration within the tripartite health system, linking clinical and general medicine with a population approach.[51] The ideal health centre, according to its proponents, could house GPs, nurses, midwives, social workers, preventive health clinics, and facilities for health education and statistical study, hence fulfilling social medicine's goal of combining research with teamwork and education.

Manchester Local Authority Health Department had drawn up its own plans for the establishment of health centres in 1943, as part of preparations for the post-war reconstruction of the city. The original intention was to have fifteen main health centres, and up to sixty subsidiary centres across the city, depending upon the development of national policy. The preparation for Manchester's scheme had involved visits to a number of existing health centres around the country, including those in the city of Bristol and the Pioneer Health Centre in Peckham, but it was clear to all that the building of new homes would take priority at the end of the war. In the event, in Manchester and elsewhere, health centres remained a 'redundant experiment' until the 1960s, stymied by the removal of planning powers from local authorities, by post-war economic restrictions, and by opposition from interested parties, including the Central Health Services Council, the British Medical Association, and the Treasury.[52]

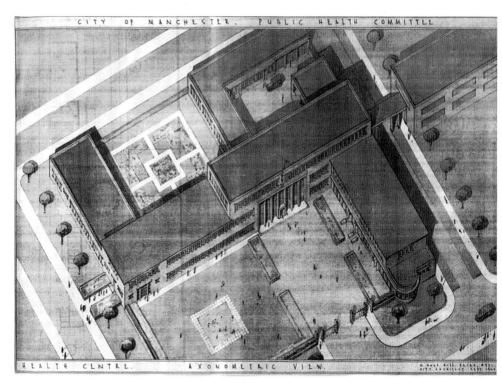

a

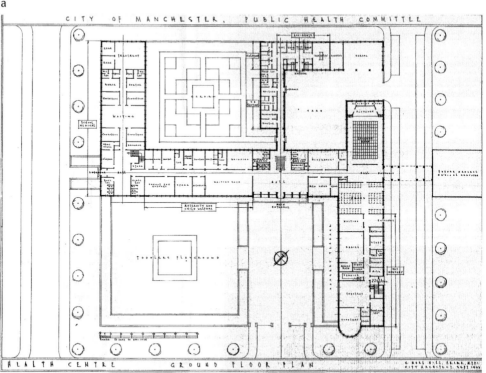

b

As became increasingly clear during and after the Second World War, most general practitioners were deeply worried by their proposed incorporation into health centres run by local authorities. Some wartime plans had already downplayed the involvement of GPs in health centres. For instance, in the 1943 plans of Manchester's Health Centre, 'future general medical services' were to be housed in a separate building, albeit connected by a walkway (see the architect's plans). The first local authority combined clinic in Manchester, amalgamating maternal and child welfare, a dental unit, and a school clinic, was opened in 1958, in the Northern Moor district, but did not contain GPs. A working committee of GPs and the City Council was set up in 1965 to consider the provision of health centres, but the MOH could only report that they had come to 'a general agreement on the principle of such establishments'.[53] It was not until the mid to late 1960s that the health centre gained greater acceptance locally and became a major instrument in the expansion of community health services nationwide; and that was largely on the initiative of GPs who no longer had much reason to fear 'encroachment' by local authorities.

When Manchester city's plans for health centres stalled, the University led the way by establishing Manchester's experimental health centre, Darbishire House, in June 1954. Again John Stopford was a key player.[54] Support for the health centre also came from Robert Platt. His hope was that urban GPs working in large health centres would become an integral part of medical schools, demonstrating to students their practical role in the community, and raising their own status in the process. Funding for the health centre came from the Nuffield Provincial Hospitals Trust (NPHT), which had strong links with the Manchester professoriate and had already funded several local developments in medicine, from the Rockefeller Foundation, and the City. It was the NPHT who bought Darbishire House, a former hostel, for £17,500.[55]

For his part, Brockington envisaged GPs and the municipal health departments as 'partners in social medicine'. He saw the relationship between the MOH and his community as resembling that between a GP and his individual patient, in that both studied the intimate life of their particular patient, and had responsibility for the preservation of that patient's health care. Indeed, in Brockington's view, the 'general practitioner should be the ally of the health department in supporting the family'; the GP, he pointed out, was closest to patients, and hence likely to notice the social, economic and epidemiological changes affecting health.[56] Brockington and his staff at the Department of Social and Preventive Medicine, played an important role in the negotiations that preceded the University Teaching Health

Centre, and in its work. Bob Logan, as a Reader, had the difficult task of liaising between the University, the health centre, and the GPs who worked there.

Later analyses suggest that the University Health Centre had mixed success. Weekly maternal and child welfare clinics were established, and provision expanded for local authority home nursing, health visiting, home helps, and social work, thereby fulfilling some of the aims of Social Medicine. But after ten years, the collaboration with the School Medical Service had ended, none of the four GPs who had re-located their inner-city practices to Darbishire House had taken up a session at the local hospital, and their involvement in group teaching had lapsed. Crucially, the Centre had produced very little research on social factors in health.[57] Dr Joyce Leeson, a graduate of the Manchester DPH and later a Senior Lecturer in the Department of Social and Preventive Medicine, remembered that the doctors at the centre often seemed unwilling to take a broader view of what they were doing. Furthermore, antagonism between academic public health staff and the GPs had grown, as had competition between the GPs and local authorities. Whilst University departments normally recruited staff keen to research and teach, the Health Centre, perhaps of necessity, had recruited GPs who happened to practise near the University.

In 1946, Metcalfe Brown had expected the NHS to strengthen links between hospitals and universities. As noted, these were already strong in Manchester where both the municipal hospitals and the charity hospitals were represented with the University on the Joint Hospital Advisory Board. One of the Board's schemes, favoured by Metcalfe Brown, was for a University Department of Child Health partly funded by the major local authorities. He also wanted co-operation in other fields of medicine, including public health, where for more than half a century, Manchester University had been noted for practical bacteriology. However, aside from its involvement in the experimental Health Centre, the Manchester Local Authority Health Department appears to have had very little to do with the University in this period. Concerned by the 'rampant' number of staff absences, the Establishment Committee of the City Council refused to allow two medical officers unpaid leave to attend the DPH course, in 1952. Metcalfe Brown was also refused leave to lecture at the University. These decisions were eventually overturned, after the Health Committee defended the DPH as 'essential qualification for the proper recruitment of medical officers of health' and 'to the ultimate benefit of the city, and to the credit and advantage of all local government'.[58]

At this time, Manchester seems to have been Britain's leading university for integration with public services. The head of Simon Engineering Ltd, Ernest Darwin Simon, and his wife Sheena, were leaders in this effort. They had both been Manchester Councillors, and Ernest played major national roles in the BBC and the University Grant Committee, providing funding for public employees to study or research at the University. But, as we have noted, some of these efforts met resistance from Manchester City Council. Their Health Department did however collaborate with the Manchester Dental School, after they were approached by Prof. Hardwick with a plan to place his students within the community. According to Dr Elizabeth Jones, Deputy Senior Medical Officer and later Deputy MOH for Manchester, who knew Prof. Hardwick and his wife personally, Hardwick wanted his students to experience the 'Moss Side mouth', i.e. the poor dental health of Caribbean mothers and their children. With Health Committee approval, two clinics were opened, including one in Moss Side, where students worked under the supervision of Local Authority dental staff. But it was Salford, Lancashire County Council and other county boroughs who actively sent their staff on the DPH course, and set up joint appointments for academic staff members. This co-operation owed much to the presence of progressive MOsH in these areas, including J. Lancelot Burn and Stanley Gawne. In Salford, Joyce Leeson carried out important work on school health, whilst Mervyn Susser served as medical officer for Mental Health.

Losses and Legislative Change

Brockington retired in 1965, but was not replaced until 1967, and this hiatus changed the direction of the department. The Chief Medical Officer, Sir George Godber, and various heads of departments around the country were consulted on their views as to possible replacements.

Their replies suggested the department could go down either of two distinct paths. The first, research, would meet the expectations of the University. The second, training for medical administration, would constitute 'a more radical departure', fulfilling the training needs of those medical students who would be necessary to fill senior posts within hospital boards, major local health authorities and the health departments of government. The latter, so-called progressive, approach, would require a 'different type of man' from the usual candidate, with the traditional Local Authority background.[59] Interestingly, both prescriptions appeared to ignore all that had gone on in the department since 1950, especially the development and teaching of Social Medicine at undergraduate and postgraduate levels, which had been considered essential for both understanding the causes of ill health, and developing effective preventive and treatment strategies.

The appointments committee appears to have had a difficult time drawing up a shortlist. Two local candidates, Mervyn Susser and Bob Logan, were seen by many as front-runners for the post. Brockington himself endorsed the appointment of Susser to the Chair, believing that his record in both local authority practice and social medicine research would make him a difficult candidate to beat. Although Susser and Logan were interviewed in 1964, they were both turned down for the post; the arrangements committee unable to come to a unanimous decision. In 1966, Mervyn Susser left Manchester for the USA where he had been a visiting researcher; he took up a Chair at Columbia University, where he and Zena Stein spent the rest of their distinguished careers. In a letter sent to Manchester's Vice-Chancellor in 1966, Susser compared the English university system, which exercised a model of 'extrusion', with the US, which was a matter of 'attraction'.[60] Susser said he had hoped to return to Manchester after a leave of absence, but not at the expense of creativity and production. Bob Logan also later left the University to become Professor of the Organisation of Medical Care at the London School of Hygiene and Tropical Medicine.

In 1967, the University finally appointed Dr Ernest Alwyn Smith as Brockington's successor. A former student of Thomas McKeown at Birmingham, Smith was committed to the social medicine model that had been established at Manchester. Indeed, he firmly believed in a reciprocal relationship between public health as a science, and as a practice, and that public health's political agenda was progressive in nature. After spending time as a WHO visiting lecturer in Singapore (1956–1958), Smith had returned to the UK and taken a post as a lecturer in public health at Queens College Dundee (1959–1961), before becoming medical statistician to the Scottish Health Department, and Senior Lecturer in the Department of

Social Medicine and Public Health at Edinburgh University. He was then appointed Director of the Social Paediatric Research Group in Glasgow, where, in collaboration with the MOH and the local authority, he put in place systems to help encourage mothers and their children to attend local authority clinics to receive treatment for rickets – still a very serious problem in Glasgow at that time.[61]

At the start of Smith's tenure, the University was expanding rapidly. The new Medical School (the Stopford Building) was built between 1969 and 1973 on the understanding that it would take on many more students. Resources were relatively unrestricted, and everyone seemed interested in Manchester being at the forefront of academic practice.[62] Smith found this a complete contrast to his experiences in Edinburgh, where many of the professors in the medical school had appeared hostile, and more likely to thwart rather than support others' plans for development. Though with the loss of Brockington, Susser, and later Logan, Smith's own department had lost some of its impetus, he continued to develop the innovative programmes of study and training. He kept up the cause of nursing education, where the opposition had now weakened. He soon persuaded the University to recognise the diploma course as a Bachelor of Nursing Degree programme.[63]

There was also a new face at the head of the Manchester City Health Department. When Metcalfe Brown retired in 1967, his successor was Dr Kennedy Campbell, MOH for the town of Paisley in Scotland. Recollections of the 'dour Scot', describe him as an introvert, increasingly unavailable to his staff, and unwilling to engage face to face with the people of Manchester, often sending his deputies to address public enquiries on such contentious issues as slum clearance. His previous experience at Paisley, some believed, prepared him badly for the problems of the larger, more diverse city. That Campbell was also appointed over the much admired and respected Deputy MOH for Manchester, Dr Anthony Essex-Cater, may also explain some of the criticism. More than one account suggests that a newly elected Conservative administration resented Essex-Cater's support of the previous Labour Council on a number of key issues. Essex-Cater left Manchester to become Medical Officer of Health for Jersey.

Between 1967 and 1970, Campbell oversaw the development of a handful of services; some already in place, others newly required by law. There was an expansion in family planning clinics, which since the early twentieth century had been run on a largely voluntary basis. (Marie Stopes, one of the founders of the family planning movement, had been a University lecturer in Palaeobotany in Edwardian Manchester, and her clinics were supported by her second husband, Humphery Roe, pilot and brother of the Manchester aircraft manufacturer, A. V. Roe.) Manchester's first local authority-run clinic opened at Moss Side Maternity and Child Welfare Centre in December 1966, under the Manchester Act. The clinic provided treatment and supplies, but only to women for whom pregnancy would be detrimental to health. The following year, the government passed the Family Planning Act (1967), which extended local authority powers to cover advice and supplies given for social as well as medical reasons. Five additional clinics were scheduled to be opened in Manchester for 1968.

The MOH Annual reports from this time show increasing co-operation between local authority nursing staff, the hospitals and general practitioners. Where possible, local authority staff were seconded to GPs, and health visitors were appointed as liaison officers in selected hospitals. In 1968, the department began a dialysis service, co-operating with the hospitals in the adaptation of patient's homes to facilitate the installation of dialysis machines. This attachment of local authority staff provided another model of health service integration, alongside the much talked about health centres which were also belatedly springing up. In 1969, Campbell also appointed four new Senior Medical Officers to cover geriatrics, family planning, health education, and pre-symptomatic diagnosis, which included responsibility for cancer screening, and the detection of metabolism defects in babies.

The growth of immigration after the Second World War presented additional burdens for the department. Medical inspections of aliens and Commonwealth migrants arriving into Manchester airport had to be carried out with ever more regularity. In 1963, all new persons arriving in the UK from a smallpox-infected area of Africa, Asia or the Americas, had to provide a valid certificate of vaccination. The medical examination, and integration of new arrivals from abroad into the community posed, the biggest problems for health departments. In 1965, Metcalfe Brown chaired a BMA working-party on the medical examination of immigrants.[64] In 1966 he appointed a liaison officer to focus on the family life and child welfare of working immigrant parents in Manchester, but she resigned before the end of the year. The Commonwealth Immigrants Act of 1968 added to the duties of Local Authorities. Afterwards, Campbell appointed a social worker and a health visitor with special responsibility for liaising with immigrants and their families.

The early 1970s brought more losses than gains for local health authorities. The Local Authority Social Services Act, 1970, and the Education (Miscellaneous Provisions) Act, 1970, transferred responsibility for day nurseries, home helps, mental health services and training centres from the Health Committee (for a short time renamed Health and Protection Committee) to the Social Services and Education Committees. In return, the health department took over administrative control of the school health service which, according to Campbell, laid 'the foundation for the creation of a true family health service, offering support from birth until death'.[65] However, there is no getting away from the fact that with the loss of the services with a significant social content, the department's responsibilities were now much reduced. An internal administrative re-organisation in 1971–1972, saw operations reduced from six to just two divisions: Environmental and Protection Health Services and Personal Health Services (see appendix 2b). The proposed Local Government Act of 1972 foreshadowed the end of the MOH role, and Campbell was already hinting that rationalisation of the department's management structure, and the introduction of management training, would ensure compatibility with the NHS.

Despite the losses, Campbell remained upbeat, seeing 'an opportunity to develop new interests in Personal and Environmental Health'.[66] But relatively little action followed the re-organisation. On family planning, for instance, Manchester was considered by the Family Planning Association to be one of a number of Councils 'dragging their feet' in terms of the quality and extent of provision.[67] As ever, mortality in the city remained relatively high in comparison to national rates (see figure 3.5).

Figure 3.5   Death rates (per 1000 persons) from all causes, Manchester Local Authority, and England and Wales, 1945–1973.

Source: Manchester MOH Reports, 1945–1973.

Campbell did oversee the final slum clearance in the city, making Manchester the first major city to complete its post-war programme of slum clearance. However, there was still a good deal of housing in the city that was far from meeting acceptable standards, even if it was not formally classified as unfit.[68] Work continued on the construction of new housing estates, including the Hulme Crescents, which consisted of continuous multi-deck blocks of flats. Hailed as the 'new Bloomsbury', the Crescents were initially a source of civic pride when they were developed at the end of the 1960s. However, poor construction, design and maintenance, including problems with lighting, refuse collection, and the cost of communal heating, resulted in worsening environmental conditions and the ill-health of tenants.[69]

Overview

This chapter on the history of local authority public health services during the early years of the NHS has shown that loss of the municipal hospitals did not lead to a period of inactivity. Yes, there were difficulties in providing the infrastructure to support new services, but national and local constraints, especially in the decade immediately after the war, gave MOsH everywhere scant room to manoeuvre.

Some pre-Second World War concerns were carried over: housing, and maternal and child welfare being the most prominent. Post-war reconstruction brought renewed efforts to promote the health and well-being of entire families, as well as the environmental conditions under which they lived. And a set of new concerns emerged: community care, especially of the elderly and the mentally ill; the specific health and welfare needs of immigrants and their families; and cancer. However, despite efforts to develop preventive services in these areas, provision was far from satisfactory, leaving challenges for future generations to resolve.

Perhaps the greatest local drive for change in public health services in this period came from academic rather than municipal leadership. Manchester University was a world leader in using social sciences towards the improvement of public services, and 'Social Medicine' had the potential to develop effective preventive and treatment strategies. In the 1950s, it pioneered a range of new programmes, some of which succeeded. In the following decades, however, the public health department would struggle to maintain its eminent position, as it faced the increasingly difficult task of balancing the demands of the University, with the needs of a re-organised health service.

CHAPTER FOUR

A Re-organised NHS, 1974–1990

T HE NHS HAD BEEN A POPULAR SUCCESS. Especially when compared with the mostly private USA, it had proved a very economical way of providing medical services for a whole population. The technical level of services had improved enormously in the first quarter-century of the NHS, without the massive cost escalation, then characteristic of insurance-based services. If reform seemed necessary, it was less because of new problems than of an opportunity to remedy problems left unsolved in 1948 – the tripartite division and the difficult relations with local authorities. That local government was going to be re-organised was a major reason for attempting a reform of the NHS, after 25 years of what, in retrospect, seems astonishing organisational stability.

The aim of reform was to make the NHS coterminous with local government. Public health clinics would be brought into the main NHS structure, and the organisational isolation of GP services would be diminished. Reform would facilitate co-ordination, and management would be improved, by organising teams of doctors, nurses, and general managers, at each level. The new system would enhance the tendency away from historical and incremental funding, and towards formula funding by population and need. There was little to quarrel with in the aims; their realisation was disastrous – as judged by onlookers and participants at the time (if not by later standards).

Partly this was the fault of the plan, but the context was also difficult. The post-war economic and political settlement was fraying, in Britain and globally. The Heath government of 1970–1974 had initially attempted a move towards economic liberalism, but had backed off and been defeated by the miners' strike. The Labour government which returned under Harold Wilson had to cope with the consequences of a major global increase in oil prices, and

British industry was being challenged by continental Europe and the Far East. Money was short, Britain was under pressure from the International Monetary Fund, and the trade unions were ultimately unwilling to settle for income moderation in the national interest. Public services were increasingly subject to cutbacks and industrial action, and the NHS was the largest and most problematic of the public services. With limited investment in the Service, and with more Britons travelling abroad and making comparisons, the NHS came to seem a relatively poor service, rather then an economical one.

In this inauspicious environment, much of 'public health' was redefined when it was pulled into the main NHS structures. Hospital services loomed larger, as environmental services moved to non-medical realms in the local authorities. Where epidemiologists had traditionally concerned themselves with infectious diseases, and expanded into the causes of chronic diseases such as lung cancer and heart conditions, now they were also to evaluate services. Public health practitioners were asked to attend less to population indicators, and more to diminishing the load on the NHS and increasing its effectiveness. That tendency has increased since the 1970s, but as we shall see, there were also counter moves, for example around the Black Report of 1980. To the annoyance of the Thatcher government, Black and his colleagues focussed on health inequalities and better overall indicators, as social goods which governments might deliver. At a time when the old populationist drivers – industrial production and fighting manpower – had disappeared, and the cost of the NHS was a very present problem, Black's concern with public health as an end in itself came as a surprise to many.

But long term aims were easily lost, as public health doctors found their work and their organisations disrupted by ever more frequent re-organisations; institutional survival often became an end in itself. Yet once in a while, during periods of relative stability, some public health workers were able to realise new visions, if only for brief periods.

The First NHS Re-organisation and its Discontents

On 1 April 1974, hospital and specialty services, local authority health services, and family practitioner services throughout the country, merged to form a single, integrated health care system. Fourteen Regional Health Authorities were established whose role was to plan across the whole health service, allocate resources, and oversee the activities of some ninety Area Health Authorities. These Area Health Authorities, whose boundaries corresponded to those of the county or metropolitan authorities (also re-organised at this time), became directly responsible for hospitals and clinics, and a variety of health services previously managed by local government, including vaccinations, health centres, family planning, school health, health visiting, and home nursing. On account of its medical school and numerous teaching hospitals, Manchester was one of nineteen area authorities designated as Area Health Authorities (Teaching) (AHA(T)). It was one of eleven areas under the North Western Regional Health Authority (NWRHA); a huge region covering a population of 4.1 million in 1974.

A third tier of the new national system comprised over two hundred District Health Teams, responsible for the day-to-day management of the hospital, specialist, and community health services. Manchester was divided into three districts: North, Central and South, roughly corresponding to the former Hospital Management Committees. Community Health Councils (CHCs) were established for each district to provide public representation, which was increasingly identified with consumer representation. Their membership was appointed by local authorities, voluntary organisations, and other community groups representing consumer interests. CHCs had no management powers, but some were openly critical of the local management of the NHS.

The 1974 re-organisation brought far-reaching changes to the way in which public health services were run. Almost overnight, the local government-based MOsH were replaced by Community Physicians, who were awarded consultant status and attached to each of the regional, area and district levels of the NHS. Public health was repackaged as 'community medicine', and given the task of easing the integration of the health services, and redirecting resources away from the hospitals and curative care and towards preventive medicine in the community. After losing some of its functions to the NHS, local government remained responsible for the environmental health function and continued to manage such services as communicable disease control, housing, clean air, pollution, food safety and meat inspection, pest control, and disinfestation.

The problems with the 1974 system were evident immediately. To begin with, the role of community medicine was poorly defined. Community Physicians were expected to fulfil multiple functions of specialist, manager and advisor, but some public health doctors working in Manchester recalled a lack of real activity and planning, and an endless round of meetings, with too much hands-on clinical work and not enough 'community diagnosis'.

The continuing economic crisis of the 1970s led to escalating health costs, and hindered the funding and expansion of health services. Locally, planned work was either postponed or abandoned, increasing dissatisfaction with the reforms. Manchester Area Health Authority's immediate priority was the hospitals, and it was only in September 1976, that the management of community services was fully de-centralised. Financial constraints and a shortage of resources meant that posts, especially those in planning and social services, were not immediately filled, and both North and South Manchester were without a District Community Physician (DCP) for significant periods of time.[1]

The NHS structure which emerged in 1974 emphasised an integrated and inclusive health service, managed through a system of consensus between managers (district administrator, district treasurer, district nursing officer, district community physician) and clinicians; a GP represented the local medical committee (of GPs), and a consultant represented the medical executive committee (of the hospital). However, it became quickly apparent that there was a considerable overlap in roles and responsibilities between the three tiers of the NHS. Family Practitioner Committees were only nominally related to AHAs and did not address GP organisational questions; and the system of consensus management proved difficult and time-consuming.

In Manchester, the public health staff who had worked for the Local Authority, from medical officers through to health visitors, found that the division of the city into three parts undermined the NHS's ability to see the city as a whole. Some missed the integrated working environment of the Town Hall, and the resulting problems of co-ordination would take decades to resolve.[2]

The defects of the 1974 re-organisation were officially recognised in the Report of the Royal Commission on the NHS in 1979. Shortly afterwards, the new Conservative government published *Patients First*, a consultative document outlining their plans for the troubled health service. The Area tier of management was to be removed, and decision-making brought as near as possible to the point of patient care.

These plans were implemented on 1 April 1982, when 192 District Health Authorities became directly responsible for defining and developing a comprehensive range of services for their communities, and for implementing strategic plans. The NWRHA held financial control, and monitored the implementation of district plans, but was to stand back from operational activities.

And so Manchester's NHS administration remained in three geographical parts. Some staff felt that continued division encouraged parochial approaches, and had hoped Manchester would become a single district. Others were pleased that the District Authorities had survived. The boundaries of North, Central and South Manchester District Health Authorities roughly matched those of the major hospitals in the city, and the District Authorities appreciated their independence. It was rumoured that the NWRHA also welcomed the new arrangement – as preventing the creation of a 'strong Manchester'.

The removal of the area tier speeded up decision-making, but it also led to greater polarisation between the management and the specialist advisor functions of the community physician. In 1984, the Griffiths management reforms led to the reconstitution of district health authority management boards, and the introduction of a system of general management. The aim was to improve lines of communication and give doctors a greater say in decision-making, but the general impression was that the status of the community physician, and the issue of community medicine as a whole had been seriously eroded by the mid 1980s. At the 1982 re-organisation, many community physicians had been forced to apply for new and fewer jobs at district level or to take early retirement, leaving many in the service demoralised. Two successive re-organisations also harmed recruitment. In 1976, fifteen per cent of community medicine posts remained unfilled. In September 1984, fifteen District Medical Officer and 188 Specialist in Community Medicine posts lay vacant.[3]

Towards the end of the decade, the emergence of high-profile communicable diseases (an outbreak of Salmonellosis at Stanley Royd Hospital in 1986; HIV/ AIDS; and BSE) seemed to confirm that public health had indeed taken its 'eye off the ball'. The resulting inquiry into the future of the public health function was led by the Chief Medical Officer, Sir Donald Acheson. The Acheson Report, published in 1988, criticised the way in which organisational and management change in the NHS had undermined public health as a specialty, and recommended the appointment of Directors of Public Health (DsPH) at all levels of the NHS to address the problems.

The NHS had returned to district authorities in 1982, after eight years of confusion between district and area functions. DsPH essentially filled the gap left by the removal of the MOH in 1974. DsPH were to provide epidemiological advice to District Health Authorities on priorities, the planning of services, and the evaluation of outcomes. They were also charged with developing and evaluating policy on prevention, health promotion and education, co-ordinating the control of communicable diseases, and acting as chief medical advisers and spokespersons for the authorities on public health matters. Crucially, DsPH were to prepare annual reports on the health of their local population, much like the MOH reports of the past.

Many scholars and practitioners have argued that the Acheson Report revived the public health function.[4] The change in title from 'Community Medicine' to 'Public Health' was welcomed by many of our informants; 'community medicine' had meant too many things to too many people. But our informants did not, on the whole, agree that prior to the Acheson reforms, public health doctors had lost control over local health and health services. In our interviews with them, they stressed the gains at local level, in the late 1970s and early 1980s, when changes in the concept of public health had led to some exceptional local innovations, both inside and outside the NHS. Some issues not yet on the national agenda, such as the role of local government and health inequalities, were not neglected locally, whilst the city also dealt with the advent of HIV/AIDS as effectively as any other.

Changes in the Concept of Public Health

As we have already seen, public health had been variously re-defined since the nineteenth century. Both 'social medicine' and 'health education' came to the fore after the Second World War. The former represented an academic, evidence-based approach to the study of health and the influence of wider determinants; the latter, a practical preventive strategy, by which individuals and groups could ideally learn to lead lives more conducive to the maintenance of health.

Within the re-organised NHS after 1974, 'community medicine' was more an occupational category than a novel public health approach; it grew closer to hospital-medicine, and shifted continually between analysis of health problems and administration of health services. Health education, remained an important element of both policy and rhetoric in this period,[5] and an important tool of the new area health authorities and local councils alike; but it was focused on individual behaviour rather than the broader context stressed by advocates of social medicine. Dissatisfaction with the seemingly narrow focus of official approaches, led some medical and health activists to develop new ideas and methodologies, including 'health promotion' and the 'new public health'.

The idea of health promotion teamed health education with health oriented public policy and improved primary care; it was developed through both national and international circles in the late 1970s, taking its cue from the radical critiques of medicine, such as Thomas McKeown's thesis that improvements in population health owed more to better diets and higher standards of living than to medical interventions. In 1977, a national Politics of Health

Group was established in London, comprising socialists, feminists, researchers, activists, and community workers with an interest in the health service. This 'radical turn' was in reaction to their exclusion from the elite public health establishment. Through meetings and publications, the group linked patterns of ill health to the unequal distribution of resources and power in society, and looked for ways in which these could be tackled through the NHS. Several books and articles were published, and the group gave rise to a number of new independent organisations, including the Women's Health Information Centre, and Radical Nurses.[6] At the international level, the 1974 Lalonde Report on the health of Canadians, and the World Health Organisation's Alma Ata Declaration in 1978, helped forge a new agenda for preventive medicine and public policies.

In Manchester, action centred on the university campus, with the formation of student-led groups, such as Community Action, and those linked with the women's health movement. Judith Emanuel, a student at the Department of Community Medicine in 1979–1981, remembers an exciting group of people, including several who would be locally prominent in the 1980s, including Joyce Leeson, Judith Gray and Carol Baxter. Inspired by the national group, Emanuel, along with some medical and nursing undergraduates, including Alistair Stewart and Mary Twomey, established a Politics of Health Group at the university.

Manchester also pioneered health promotion as an academic discipline and professional vocation. When the Health Education Council (HEC) began looking into the possibility of training people in health education and health promotion, Manchester established an M.Sc. programme. It was led by lecturer Leo Baric, who had been director of the Health Education Institute in his native Croatia before joining the Christie Hospital Social Research Unit in 1963 to study the acceptance of cervical smear tests. Grounded in the 'holistic' European system of public health, Baric wanted to put the action into public health in the UK. Community medicine, he felt, had come to mean mainly epidemiology. Instead of simply identifying health problems, Baric was concerned with solutions.

The two-year, part-time course established at Manchester covered sociology, psychology and research methods, with a strong focus on evidence-based work, impact assessment and evaluation. The course accommodated people from a variety of backgrounds, looking for various careers around public health. A number of the graduates went on to the newly created health education posts within the NHS and the Local Authority. The involvement of non-medics in what was still very much a medicalised field of activity continued a trend in Manchester which would strengthen throughout the following decades.

While researching the social aspects of health and illness, including the influence of social norms and social roles, Baric formulated his 'Social Intervention Model of Health Education' (SIM) in 1979. Based upon a distinction between decision-making and normative behaviour, this model of population-based intervention argued that it was easier to promote better health and prevention through influencing and changing social norms, than through changing an individual's behaviour. Applying this model to the issue of smoking, he argued for a focus on non-smokers who had yet to acquire the habit, and in reducing the areas where smoking was still acceptable.[7] This approach entered national policy during the late 1970s and early 1980s.[8] The British Medical Association accused Baric of trying to bring socialism in by the back door,[9] but he and his Manchester colleagues did much to secure academic recognition of health education and health promotion, and international recognition of SIM.

By the 1980s, an approach soon labelled 'the new public health' was developing in Britain. As noted, it combined health promotion with an understanding of the environmental determinants of health, and was again greatly influenced by the international health scene. In 1981, the WHO European Office launched its 'Health For All by the Year 2000' strategy, which set thirty-eight targets to improve the health and well-being of disadvantaged groups, covering many aspects of care, the environment, and public policy. Key features of the Health For All programme included the reallocation of health resources from tertiary care to community-based primary care, healthy public policies, multisectoral working, and community participation. In the mid 1980s, the WHO European Office also began promoting the Healthy Cities Initiative, created in part by Dr John Ashton in Liverpool. A network of urban health promotion initiatives promoted the Health For All strategy. By 1988, there were twenty-four European project cities, including four in Britain: Bloomsbury/Camden, Liverpool, Belfast and Glasgow.

A Health For All working party was set up in Manchester, combining the City Council, the Health Authorities and the voluntary sector, but the impact appears to have been marginal, as in most other British cities. Not until 1996 did Manchester obtain Healthy City status (some eight years after its north-west neighbour, Liverpool), but it was in a European network for developing urban strategies and facilitating research. And as we will see, health promotion and Health For All objectives were implicit in many of the services rolled out locally in this period.

The NHS and the 'New Public Health': North Manchester Health Authority

After the dust had settled on the second re-organisation within a decade, the 1980s proved a period of relative administrative stability within the NHS. While the hospital agenda and the treatment of the sick continued to dominate national policy and consume a large chunk of health authorities' time, effort and resources, sustained prevention at the local level was eventually able to get under way. Of Manchester's three Health Authorities, North Manchester stands out for the way in which it re-thought its pattern of care, and developed policies and services to meet the new public health agenda.[10]

North Manchester's approach was underpinned by recognition of the huge health problems of the district, including some of the worst health inequalities in the city. That many of the hospital buildings were in a poor state of repair added to the generally depressed state of the local community. The 'new public health' in North Manchester was about raising low expectations, and giving access to healthier lives.

The North Manchester Public Health Department was led by District Medical Officer Dr Joyce Leeson, who moved to North Manchester from the South District at the 1982 re-organisation, and stayed until the early 1990s. The continuity within the Department, and at Board and senior management level, was unparalleled in Manchester. In other districts, public health positions were left vacant as people moved on in the late 1980s.

A former student and member of staff at the University of Manchester Department of Social and Preventive Medicine, Leeson was a political radical and feminist, committed to the social medicine approach. She had left the University after failing to gain the public health chair, and in North Manchester, she fronted a public health department of like-minded professionals, many of whom were also connected with the University. They included Drs Judith Gray (mental health services), Peter Elton (community services), and Di Chisholm. Judith Emanuel was District Health Promotion Officer, and later head of the Health Promotion Unit within the Public Health Department; and there were 'some very good community nurses, district nurses and health visitors'.[11]

North Manchester Public Health Department embraced the 'Health For All' approach and was particularly successful at encouraging intersectoral working with the Local Authority, local communities and voluntary organisations. After the AIDS crisis in the mid 1980s, the department worked with South and Central Health Promotion Units, the Local Education Authority, and other groups, to get personal, social, and sexual health education into local authority schools. It also piloted the first 'Healthbank'. Still in existence today, Healthbank encourages NHS employees to address their health concerns and improve their skills and knowledge.

With the shift to 'care in the community' in the 1980s, money became available for the resettlement of asylum patients.[12] North Manchester established networks of social support through the Resettlement Teams (for people with mental health problems), the Community Support Team (for people with learning difficulties), and the Community Drug Team. Screening programmes and walk-in clinics were established for various groups and localities which were underprivileged or overlooked, including the elderly, and men. The Chair of the Regional Health Authority was even encouraged to make an annual visit to the Well Men Clinic.

Poster advertising 'Healthbank' in North Manchester. North Manchester Public Health Annual Report, 1991.

North Manchester had had an ethnically diverse community from the late nineteenth century. By the 1970s, it included substantial Jewish, Eastern European, Pakistani and African-Caribbean populations. In the 1980s, staff from North Manchester, including those who were themselves Muslim, worked with the Pakistani community on various health issues specific to them, including vitamin D deficiency and rickets, nutrition, diet and obesity. As part of a Chinese health initiative to reach a community generally dispersed across the city, a health information centre was set up above a restaurant in China Town. With a Chinese worker alongside the department's own health visitors, the information centre provided dietary advice and educational talks about how to use health services.

North Manchester Women's Health Team

North Manchester Health Authority prided itself on doing things a little differently, not least in its approach to women's health. The North Manchester Women's Health Team was established in 1985, spearheaded by Joyce Leeson and Judith Gray, both of whom had been instrumental in the setting-up of a Well Women Clinic in South Manchester. The North Manchester Team was the first such permanently embedded specialist NHS service in the UK, providing a radical approach to preventive health care for women, incorporating the aims and philosophies of the women's health movement.[13]

For a long time, the Women's Health Team fought to justify its existence in the face of NHS cuts to preventive services. Originally run as part of the Health Promotion Unit in North Manchester, it became a mainstream community service in 1987, with its own budget provided by Urban Aid money and the Health Authority. A District Planning Group for Women's Health Services was established under the chair of the District Medical Officer, which placed women's health needs firmly within senior NHS structures.[14]

By the beginning of 1991, North Manchester had five Well Women Centres/Clinics with a sixth one due to open that October. Each clinic was run according to the specific needs of its neighbourhood. Unlike the Well Women clinics in South Manchester which tended to be led by health visitors, and the clinically-orientated practices in Central Manchester, North Manchester's clinics followed a self-empowerment model. In other words, they actively sought to give local women, and other workers and agencies, a direct say in the planning and development of their services. This 'self-help' approach was similar to that adopted in other areas of the country, including Liverpool.[15] Though the services of woman doctors were provided, the centres/clinics tended to depart from the medical model, and to focus on personal development for local people.

The Women's Health Team worked with older women, women with disabilities, Asian women and young women, all of whom had proved relatively reluctant to access these services. After requests from over-60s groups, training was offered in exercise and relaxation. A 'Health Fair and Festival' was held in Newton Heath to obtain the views of the over-60s on the services they wanted. Physical access to community services was made easier; and the Team liaised with the voluntary sector, care groups and other relevant associations to hold a Carers Fair. An 'A-Z' for Carers was published with the support of North Manchester Community Health Council.

In the Cheetham Hill area of North Manchester, women workers and activists from the large, non-white population had already been campaigning for a Well Women Centre. They quickly made their demands known to the Women's Health Team, and, after a nine-month consultation and planning period, a Health Day and two health courses were organised. Further health courses were led by women within the Asian community, and an Asian women's health worker was appointed for outreach and development. This work led to the establishment of Neesa, an Asian Women's Health Project with its own designated worker. Neesa is still running and now has three workers.[16]

Finally, the Women's Health Team helped to establish Y-WAIT (Young Women's Health, Advice, Information and Time to talk), a service for women under the age of twenty-five, who rarely attended the existing Well Women clinics, family planning services, and antenatal classes. With the support of the Regional Health Authority and some short-term HIV/AIDS funding, around twenty female volunteers (many of them teenage mothers) were trained on issues such as contraception, drugs, and sexuality. These young women then counselled and supported others through a weekly drop-in session, at which a doctor and a family planning nurse were provided by the Health Authority. Y-WAIT consulted young women and girls on the services they wanted, and maintained contact with local agencies, including the Probation Service, the Youth Service, and the Community Drugs Team. In April 1991, Y-WAIT became independent, with a financial award of £15,000 per year for three years from Joint Finance, which also enabled the service to employ a part-time worker, and cover their running costs. (Though it served as a model for this type of initiative across the country, Y-WAIT no longer exists.)

The success of the North Manchester Public Health Department owed much to the support it received from senior management and the Health Authority Board, particularly its Chair, Professor Joe Moore, and its General Manager/Chief Executive, Mike Brown. Moore was a professor of dentistry who had previously been Dean of the Manchester Medical School. Before his appointment to North Manchester, Brown had held a series of administrative posts in the NHS, most recently at University College Hospital in London. Though neither had much experience of public health and community services, they focussed on community and public health challenges in re-thinking the district's services. North Manchester staff were allowed space to innovate, and the Public Health Department was keen to experiment. Much later, Moore brought Judith Emanuel, as Director of Health Promotion, onto the Health Authority Board as an executive member, to ensure that the implications of policies and measures for poverty in the district were at least discussed at Board meetings – a move which was unique to Manchester at the time.

Moore also ensured that the Board and senior management conducted regular visits to the district's hospitals and clinics. This 'walking of the ship' – which Moore picked up from his wartime service in the navy – made the management visible, and allowed them to listen to staff, patients and the community. Visits could prove a revelation, as when Moore found a dead rat behind a fridge on a ward. In the wake of the privatisation of hospital cleaning services, this discovery led to a tightening up of practices. 'Walking the ship' also helped North Manchester to overcome the difficult industrial relations it had suffered since its inception, including one of the country's first nurses strikes.

The north of Manchester had suffered an historical lack of capital investment. With no major teaching hospital, the District was a low priority for re-development in the 1980s. Furthermore, since regional allocation was weighted in favour of age of population not deprivation, North Manchester also suffered in as much as its death rates in middle-age were relatively high.

Moore and his team cultivated good relations with the key regional staff, to promote a wider understanding of the poor health status of North Manchester. They also began a rationalisation of hospitals, beginning with the smaller, 'relatively low activity' hospitals. Closing the former 'community hospitals' – Ancoats and the Jewish Hospital – and the former isolation hospital at Monsall, released funds which were then channelled back into public health. North Manchester also secured a mortgage-like bridging loan from the Regional Health Authority – to start a major hospital improvement at the North Manchester General, and to help improve community-based services.

Special monies were often used to fund a public health project for three to five years, after which the costs were picked up by the Health Authority. In hindsight, Brown recalled that the Public Health Department were not particularly demanding of Health Authority funds. In a tough economic climate, Leeson and her team became adept at milking other sources of funding, including joint finance pots and Inner Cities money. Their achievement in community services and health promotion suggested that substantial funding was not always necessary to make a substantial difference, at least in terms of morale, education and access.

The Public Health Department's 'tried and tested' model of dialogue with concerned communities proved instrumental in contests around the issue of hospital rationalisation. The closure of the Ancoats A&E department, for instance, produced a major backlash within the local community, including a sit-in at the department. Staff of the Public Health Department involved themselves in a dialogue with community representatives, as well as making the A&E staff at Crumpsall Hospital part of the planning process. As a result, a Walk-In-Clinic was established to deal with minor injuries and other health issues, many of which had previously been seen at the A&E department. The A&E Consultant, Dr Phil Randall, trained the nursing staff in wound management and minor injuries, and provided telephone support to the clinic.

North Manchester Health Authority liaised with local GPs at every stage to ensure they were providing a complementary service, and the ambulance service provided transport back-up for walk-in patients requiring emergency treatment. Indeed, the transition of

Table 4.1   Health and social data for early 1980s Manchester.

Area*	SMR All Causes, All Persons, Under 65 Years, 1981–1983	SMR All Persons, Coronary Heart Disease, 1981–1983	SMR All Persons, Lung Cancer, 1981–1983	SMR All Persons, Respiratory Diseases, 1981–1983	% Male Unemployment, (Aged 16–64), 1981	% Head of Household is Unskilled, 1981	% No Car Population (Non pensioners), 1981	Low weight births, as a % of all births, 1978–1983	Child Accident rate per 1000, 1981–1983
Manchester	137	143	165	147	20.9	7.8	47.5	9.9	2.62
REM. GMC	116	131	120	124	12.7	5.5	29.1	7.8	–
Eng. & Wales	100	100	100	100	11.1	4.5	24.3	7.2	–
North A	135	148	146	170	17.4	4.5	42.9	9.4	1.77
North B	145	150	180	135	20.1	8.6	49.1	9.4	3.47
North C	173	171	216	169	26.1	10.7	61.7	10.5	4.16
Central A	178	154	213	214	33.2	11.4	70.2	12.3	3.00
Central B	150	133	151	199	24.3	9.8	49.6	10.8	3.24
Central C	130	133	181	151	17.3	6.4	44.4	10.1	2.75
South A	130	145	139	166	17.6	5.1	36.0	8.7	1.54
South B	103	121	91	81	13.3	5.3	29.6	7.1	2.21
South C	112	125	153	100	16.3	5.4	35.4	8.7	1.05
South D	142	146	173	163	23.4	10.4	51.4	9.6	2.43

* North A: Crumpsall, Blackley, Charlestown; North B: Cheetham, Harpurhey, Lightbowne, Moston; North C: Central, Newton Heath, Beswick and Clayton, Bradford; Central A: Hulme, Moss Side, Ardwick; Central B: Fallowfield, Rusholme, Longsight; Central C: Gorton North, Gorton South, Levenshulme; South A: Whalley Range, Chorlton, Barlow Moor, Old Moat; South B: Withington, Burnage, Didsbury; South C: Brooklands, Northenden, Sharston; South D; Baguley, Benchill, Woodhouse Park.

the Ancoats A&E Department into a Walk-In-Clinic for the local community seems a 'good example of broad-based involvement'.[17] A similar dialogue attended the closure of the Jewish Hospital, and the kosher meal service was relocated to the Northern Hospital with the support of Jewish religious leaders.

In September 1988, North Manchester Health Authority was named winner in the 'Best of Health Competition', a national inquiry into the NHS launched by *The Sunday Times*.[18] Ministers especially praised the health authority for implementing so many changes in spite of the adverse economic and industrial conditions. A number of the public health initiatives in North Manchester remained unique, their influence extending little beyond the district, either because they were not taken-up city-wide, or they became diluted without the creative support they had received in the North. Successive NHS re-organisations and policy changes have also brought an end to some of the more long-standing schemes, including the women's health initiatives using non-medical approaches. That said, much of the work that took place in North Manchester was exemplary of the broader trends in public health, which would continue to develop in the decades that followed, including better information gathering about local health needs, a multidisciplinary approach, and community involvement.

The particular success of public health in North Manchester had two main causes. Firstly, there were individuals, including several 'emigrants'

Table 4.2   Comparative health data for Manchester 1981–1983 and 1987–1991.

Area* (see table 4.1)	SMR All causes of death, Males under 65 years		SMR All causes of death, Females under 65 years		Low weight births, as a percentage of all births	
	1981–1983	1987–1991	1981–1983	1987–1991	1978–1983	1987–1991
Manchester	140	158	132	143	9.9	8.98
REM. GMC/NWRHA	117	113	114	111	7.8	7.40
Eng. & Wales	100	100	100	100	7.2	6.90
North A	133	160	138	162	9.4	8.47
North B	149	165	144	141	9.4	7.98
North C	184	200	152	162	10.5	10.57
Central A	182	208	169	205	12.3	10.14
Central B	149	159	152	157	10.8	10.17
Central C	135	151	123	144	10.1	8.15
South A	130	130	131	119	8.7	8.72
South B	115	131	85	106	7.1	7.42
South C	106	142	121	125	8.7	7.86
South D	138	167	150	156	9.6	8.64

Source: Heath Inequalities and Manchester (1986) and *Health Inequalities and Manchester in the 1990s* (1993).

from the medical school, who possessed vision, drive and leadership skills. Secondly, the district enjoyed an increasingly rare 'stability' in terms of organisational structure and personnel. This allowed continuity in policy, encouraged a deeper understanding of local health needs over time, and gave space for the creation, acceptance and evaluation of new services. Of course, it is difficult to demonstrate the precise impact of these efforts on mortality or morbidity in the district. As tables 4.1 and 4.2 indicate, by the end of the decade, the health gap between North Manchester and other parts of the city, and between Manchester and the country as a whole, was as wide as ever.

Health and the City Council after 1974

With the removal of community-based health services to the NHS in 1974, the City Council's responsibilities in respect of health appeared significantly reduced. That said, local government was still accountable for environmental health services, including food inspection, hygiene and safety, housing, occupational health, pollution control, airport health, pest and rodent control, veterinary services, the investigation and control of notifiable diseases, city mortuaries, and disinfestation.

The period after 1974 was one of financial retrenchment in local government generally, leading to chronic staff shortages. Training budgets were cut and purchasing of equipment reduced. Improvement across services was inevitably held back. Nevertheless, the newly appointed Director of Environmental Health for Manchester City Council, Eric W Foskett, remained upbeat, seeing the period of standstill as a challenge towards the better use of resources, to which the department could respond by taking a broad view of the environmental problems encountered in the city.[19] Despite cut backs, Manchester's Environmental Health Department was one of the largest in England, with over 300 members of staff.[20] Many of the department's chief officers were extremely well qualified, some with Ph.Ds. Foskett was regarded nationally and internationally as a leader in environmental public health.

A substantial part of the department's work was concerned with housing, especially multiple occupations, and the rehabilitation of existing stock. In his annual reports, Foskett emphasised the 'importance of housing in the health and welfare of the public … because of the amount of time each person spends in the domestic environment'.[21] The 'worrying persistence' of TB in the city, a disease long associated with sub-standard housing, was one reason for their focus.[22] The prevalence of non-respiratory TB, especially among new immigrants, much of which it was felt went unreported by consultants, also caused concerned. By 1980, three specialist health visitors had been appointed to provide information on the social background of sufferers, to follow up defaulters and to make arrangements for the screening of families and their close contacts.[23] At around this time, tenants began to react against the poor quality, management and safety of Manchester's deck-access housing estates. In 1975, the combined efforts of the Hulme Tenants' Association and leading Liberal councillors led to a major reassessment of the Hulme Crescents, resulting in the Labour-run Council agreeing to re-house all families with children above the ground floor in Hulme and in four other such estates.[24] (It would take over another decade before the multi-deck housing estates would begin to receive the re-development demanded by their residents (see next chapter).)

In 1974, the department had also taken on responsibility for home safety and health education, functions that were concurrent with the Area Health Authority. An Education and Research branch of the department was created to co-ordinate these new duties. In the 1970s, food hygiene, food-borne disease, and standards of food premises were the target of health education. In 1977, a major exhibition on home safety was held in conjunction with the other local authorities of Greater Manchester, and a year later, a mobile unit was established to further promote these activities. The department took its home safety role very seriously. The 1979 Royal Commission on the NHS had stressed the importance of health education to the prevention of ill health, and the greater effectiveness of the NHS. The department, however, believed the practical application of home safety to be even more pertinent in that 'each accident which is avoided reduces the need for subsequent medical care and attention'.[25]

The re-organisation liberated environmental health from the medical model of the MOH and enhanced the status of its officers. But they still needed to draw on medical advice, especially for re-housing priorities, immunisation and vaccination, communicable diseases, and port-health, including checks on immigrants. (Though Manchester was no longer a sea port, its airport had greatly expanded.)

Manchester's arrangements for co-ordination were unusual: the Medical Officer for Environmental Health (MOEH), though an NHS employee, worked full-time in the Environmental Health Department at the Town Hall. The DCP for Central Manchester, the former Deputy MOH, Dr Elizabeth Jones, was the first to undertake this demanding role. She had a special interest in immunisation, and spent a significant proportion of her time trying to increase uptake among poorer families in the city.

From 1984 to 1985, the general environmental health section was remodelled to include more comprehensive services in health education and home safety. This was part of a wider process of modernisation at the City Council, which now included a younger set of councillors determined to change the ways in which council services were developed and delivered. The new Council leader was Graham Stringer, and for a time, John Nicholson was 'the articulate and charismatic face of local socialism'.[26] Under the slogan 'Defending Jobs, Improving Services', they embarked on a radical programme in which health and environment were to play an important role. The new Chair of the Environmental Services Committee was Keith Bradley, who later became an MP (as did Stringer), a Minister, and later a Lord. The newly appointed Director of Environmental Health, Michael Eastwood, remembers Bradley's enthusiasm for renewal. In his last annual report as Director, Foskett had expressed his happiness that the term 'health', as used in the department's title, was again being actively promoted.[27]

Initially set on opposing the Thatcher government, the Council was forced to accommodate to the increasing centralisation of power over local developments. After Labour lost the 1987 election, Manchester leaders realised that hopes for regeneration in Manchester rested on collaboration with Tory initiatives around urban renewal, led at that time by Michael Heseltine, who at one stage was, *inter alia*, the Minister for Liverpool. Compared with its traditional local rival, Manchester's history was a gentler transition from antagonism to accommodation.

In 1986, the Council created two new posts of health campaign worker, and public health doctor specialising in housing, health and health inequalities. In line with the objectives of the 'Black Report Initiative', the post-holders began working on policy development at a national level with colleagues from other local authorities, and with Healthy City Networks in Camden, Liverpool, Leeds, and Sheffield. Much time was spent focusing on health education and health promotion in its widest sense, creating 'local consensus' on work which could make a difference to health inequalities. A year later, a Health Promotion Unit was embedded within the Environmental Health Department. The unit evolved from the Education and Research Section, and it took the corporate lead on health promotion, food hygiene, air pollution, and health.

Part of the Thatcher government's attack on local socialism was the abolition of the Metropolitan County Councils, which had been established in 1974. The Greater Manchester County Council (GMCC) had covered Salford, Stockport, Bolton, Wigan, Bury, Rochdale, Oldham, Tameside and Trafford, as well as the city itself. When the GMCC was abolished in 1986, many of its functions were devolved to the Metropolitan Boroughs, but some were retained as

CITY HEALTH

ISSUE NO. 1
SPRING 1987

MANCHESTER CITY COUNCIL
HEALTH BULLETIN

This bulletin is all about health issues which affect you and all people who live and work in Manchester. You can choose whether you wish to have future issues delivered direct to your home or to pick them up from your local library or Council office.

The Leader of Manchester City Council, Councillor Graham Stringer, says: "This first issue of 'City Health' marks the deep concern of Manchester City Council for the health of local people. The City Council is determined to do all it can to improve people's health, to provide better housing and social services and to make Manchester a healthier place in which to live and work."

In this issue we focus on the closure of Accident and Emergency provision at Ancoats Hospital. The City Council shares the dismay of local people about this closure and recognises the worries of Manchester residents about casualty services right across the city. To find out your views we have included a questionnaire, which we hope you will fill in and return. We will take account of all your opinions in our discussions with the Health Authorities.

"We need a fully operational hospital and casualty unit," says Action Group member Maggie Law. "Without it there will be deaths."

More than 35,000 patients passed through Ancoats casualty last year and in an area with a high proportion of children and elderly people, the fear for the effects on their lives is real.

In an area where many people are out of work, emergency illnesses and accidents at home have already meant paying taxi fares to hospitals further afield.

"You can't stand for an hour in the bus queue with a child that is bleeding," says local resident Christine Vernon. "Unemployed people have had to pay £7 to get to a hospital and back."

Over the last year casualty provision aross the whole city has suffered, with closure at Salford Royal and temporary closures at Withington and Manchester Royal Infirmary due to staff and bed shortages.

Casualty In the City

"By Monday I don't have any money left. If one of the children got ill on a Monday, I'd have to wait until I got my Family Allowance before I could get them to hospital."

This is the stark reality of cuts in the health service for the thousands of people who live in and around Ancoats. They have seen their hospital run down and their casualty department closed on February 1st after the Royal College of Surgeons said it could no longer recognise it as suitable for training junior doctors. The Health Authority calls is a "temporary closure" while a full public consultation is carried out.

1828-1987
Already the Ambulance Service and other hospitals are finding it difficult to cope and the new casualty department planned for North Manchester General Hospital (Crumpsall) has not been started yet.

Local people began a sit-in as soon as news of the closure broke, they are determined to stay there until it reopens, and have formed ANCOATS HOSPITAL ACTION GROUP.

federal services, led by particular Boroughs. Manchester City took over trading standards, on behalf of the other councils, and much of this work had a direct bearing on public health. Under the new title of Environmental Health and Consumer Protection, the Manchester department protected against substandard or dangerous goods, provided a credit advisory service for low-income residents who had got into debt, and tried to reduce underage sales of cigarettes and alcohol. The department also took responsibility for the management of the Greater Manchester Scientific Services, providing chemical analysis of food, water, waste and pollution samples, and giving scientific advice for the whole conurbation.

In the spring of 1987, the City Council published its first edition of *City Health;* four more followed, the last appearing in Spring 1990. The launch volume was largely concerned with the closure of Ancoats A&E Department, and general staffing cuts in the NHS. Attacks on the 'cuts' were matched by news of initiatives, including Well Woman provision, community care, health inequalities work and the city's handling of HIV/ AIDS. One might say that in the mid 1980s, the radicals on the city council were in dialectical exchange with those employed by the NHS in North Manchester – which included Graham Stringer's ward.

The Health Inequalities Debate

An important spur to public health action in Manchester was the health inequalities debate, focussed by the Black Report in 1980. Its lead author, Sir Douglas Black, was President of the Royal College of Physicians and had been for many years Professor of Medicine in Manchester, where he had initially been second in command to Robert Platt. Black's report was planned under the Labour government of James Callaghan, prompted by sociologists and social medicine specialists in London (rather than Manchester). It was reluctantly published under the Conservative government which came to power in 1979.[28] The report outlined the manifest inequalities in health experiences across the country, and stressed the close link between ill health, low income and deprivation. That substantial public expenditure was needed to reduce the widening gap between the poorest and wealthiest in terms of health, was not a message the Thatcherites wanted to hear. In a bid to distance itself from the report, the Department of Health released it on an August Bank Holiday under restricted circulation. This suppression brought notoriety, and republication. Though in the short term the report had little impact on national policy, in the long term it inspired a culture of research and debate, which grew over the following decades.[29]

Manchester responded to the Black Report by launching its own 'Black Report Initiative', undertaken jointly by the City Council and the Health Authorities. The initiative aimed at 'preventing ill-health, rather than curing it'. The Manchester Joint Consultative Committee produced its own report on *Health Inequalities in Manchester* in 1986. Even the words were sensitive – the Thatcher government notoriously avoided the term 'inequalities', referring instead to 'variations in health'. The original title of the local report, 'Health Inequalities *in* Manchester', was changed to 'Health Inequalities *and* Manchester'.

As the report made clear, Mancunians were more likely to die prematurely than their fellow countrymen, with a huge excess of deaths due to lung cancer, respiratory disease, and coronary heart disease (see again, tables 4.1. and 4.2 above). Worst off in terms of health were those living within the 'Inner Area' of the city (comprising the poor private housing and council estates of Central Manchester and most of North Manchester), together with those in the southern parts of Wythenshawe. In the Hulme, Ardwick and Moss Side area, for example, there were eighty per cent more deaths occurring within the population aged sixty-five and under, than might have been expected from national rates. (By contrast, in the more affluent areas of South Manchester, deaths of women aged below sixty-five were fifteen per cent *lower* than if national rates had applied.)[30] There was also concern over the high percentages of low birth weights and childhood accidents among the less affluent of the population.

The writers of the report acknowledged that many of the factors which contributed to health inequalities had their roots in the social structure, such as distribution of income and unemployment, about which little could be done locally. The City Council and the three Health Authorities committed themselves to tackling behaviours associated with inequality, including the promotion of healthy-eating, the combating of smoking, and the reduction of accidents in the home. The City Council, for example, launched a smoke cessation programme, in collaboration with the health authorities and the local branch of ASH (Action on Smoking and Health), targeting council employees, workplaces, and schools across the city. The Council signed up to its own Smoke Free programme, with the local NHS public health departments co-ordinating support for those council employees wishing to give up the habit. Eastwood recalls that for a short while Manchester even had one completely smoke-free restaurant and one smoke-free pub.

HIV/AIDS

The advent of HIV/AIDS provoked a major public health crisis in the UK. Between 1982 and June 1990, there were 142 reported cases of AIDS, and eighty-four recorded deaths in the NWRHA area alone.[31] As historian Virginia Berridge points out, the early responses to AIDS came as 'self-help', from locally based groupings of gay men whose 'grass roots' activism drove the formation of national policy.[32] In the early to mid 1980s, in cities across the UK, groups of gay men established helplines, held meetings, and pressed for funding to help respond to the potential crisis threatened by the disease. With its large gay community, focussed on the Canal Street district, Manchester was one of the main regional centres for AIDS activism and work. Here, as elsewhere, the politics of AIDS was built on the prior politics of Gay Liberation.

In 1985, a gay men's health group set up AIDSline, a voluntary telephone helpline, funded by a small grant from Manchester City Council. They also began exerting pressure on the health services to provide testing. The MOEH responsible was Dr Mike Painter, and much of the early testing was carried out at Withington Hospital, where the local Public Health Laboratory Service was based. Volunteers from AIDSline provided counselling at the evening testing clinics. Other voluntary groups included a North West branch of the national organisation, Body Positive, Healthy Gay Manchester, and later, Mainliners, which provided a befriending and hospital visiting scheme. Manchester became known as one of the few places outside London with good quality testing and confidential services.

As elsewhere, initial clinical treatment of infected persons exhibited a 'panic station' mentality. For instance, the nursing of infected persons centred on isolation and extraction ventilation, whilst in September 1985, the City Council went to court to obtain a magistrates order, under the Public Health Act, to detain an HIV-infected person at Monsall Hospital.

The actions of the Council were met with anger and upset in Manchester, not least among the gay community. Reactions were widely reported in local and national newspapers. Afterwards, the left-wing Council altered its approach, and began to look at ways in which such regulations could not be used again. The use of the Public Health Act was condemned by the Gay Information Centre as 'unnecessary, scaremongering and counter-productive'.[33] The Council also spoke of the need 'to eliminate the massive mythology about this disease which makes it difficult to treat AIDS on a strictly medical basis.'[34] In 1986, the Council produced one of the first AIDS policies in the country calling for greater sympathy towards the needs of young people with the disease. They also threatened to discipline any council employee discriminating against a fellow worker. The Council's change of attitude and the publication of the charter proved divisive. Health service chiefs, led by Councillor Ken Collis, Chair of Central Manchester Health Authority, accused the Council of bowing to pressure from the Gay lobby.[35] The trade unions were also critical that the safety of their members and their families was being jeopardised.[36] Eastwood recalled reactions to the launch of the AIDS charter:

> Some of the popular press of the day were highly critical of the Council and reported somewhat negatively on what was a positive public health response to a major emerging issue. Within weeks I was receiving requests from my equivalents across the country and even internationally for copies and permission to use the material within their areas.

Monsall General Hospital contained the Regional Unit for Infectious Disease, and thus North Manchester quickly became the North West's main source of diagnosed cases of AIDS. By an oddity of boundaries, the North district also included the Gay Village in central Manchester, so it was doubly involved. In 1989 to 1990 twelve out of twenty-one new cases diagnosed were residents in the North District, with the rest living further afield. By December 1990, Monsall was looking after 140 people infected with HIV or AIDS, of which fifty regularly attended the wards and out-patient clinics for prophylactic treatment.[37] The Monsall Team, which included an infection control nurse, counsellors, a social worker, a clinical psychologist and an occupational therapist, provided emotional support and care in the community for people with AIDS, working closely with all the voluntary groups.

Designation as the Regional Infectious Diseases Unit certainly focused the service management of North Manchester. However, as Joyce Leeson points out, their real aim was to show that good HIV/ AIDS services, with counselling and support, could be provided in every district, so that there would be no need for regional units or a high security infection control setting.

As well as detection and treatment, the early focus for HIV/ AIDS in Manchester was on primary prevention through health education and health promotion. An AIDS Forum and working group was convened in Manchester in late 1985, bringing together AIDSline, Local Authority representatives (as the biggest employer in the city), and a range of health service staff. In 1986, the AIDS in Education Group, described by one member as 'an example of collaborative work involving health promotion, AIDSline and local authority staff working together with no independent budget', trained people to deliver in-service training on HIV/AIDS in schools. When this training was held in May 1986, almost every school in the city was represented.

The emergence of HIV, and the danger of infection among drug-users from contaminated injection equipment, gave rise to a harm reduction approach in the UK. Here, clean injecting equipment, the supply of known doses of clean drugs, and anonymous HIV testing were provided, whilst outreach workers went into communities to inform and attract people to the services. This approach was first pioneered in Liverpool, where, unlike Manchester, it became clear that drug users, not homosexual and bisexual men, were going to be the important gateway for the virus to the wider community.[38] District Community Drugs Teams in Manchester maintained needle exchange schemes, and supported other such schemes operated from pharmacies and clinics throughout the city.

In 1986, the Department of Health and Social Security finally bowed to pressure from voluntary organisations, scientists and public health clinicians, by issuing its own advice, encouraging voluntary sector participation in local services and planning. A year later, the Regional Health Authority agreed to fund three workers attached to AIDSline for three years, and the City Council used part of its government AIDS Support Grant to fund a further two posts. By 1989, AIDSline had gained Health Authority agreement to fund an HIV worker in every community drugs team, and by the beginning of the 1990s, construction was underway to provide a permanent base for AIDSline, its counselling and outreach work, George House (later George House Trust).[39] The success achieved by Manchester in AIDS education and prevention throughout the North West was recognised by the government, and the city was awarded £709,000 from the Department of Health towards combating AIDS – over twice the amount of money allocated to other cities such as Birmingham, Liverpool, and Leeds.

The service response to HIV/AIDS in Manchester revealed the fruitfulness of working to the Health For All model. HIV/AIDS services included a wide range of staff, a participative and empowering mode of work, intersectoral planning, user group involvement and a programme of health education and prevention. As Leeson later wrote: 'Community participation and intersectoral collaboration *did* work and did make a tremendous contribution to high quality health care for a stigmatised group'.[40]

Black and Minority Ethnic Health

The 1980s also saw greater attention paid to the health needs of black and minority ethnic (BME) communities, in Manchester and beyond. Manchester has a long history of immigration, and has a significant BME population; in 2004, the Office for National Statistics estimated that there were around 96,000 people in Manchester from non-white ethnic groups. Over time, health services adapted to meet the specific needs of ethnic groups, including translation services, health centres (e.g. Chinese Health Information Centre), and targeted clinical provision in the community (e.g. the Manchester Diabetes Centre, and the Sickle Cell and Thalassaemia Centre).[41] In the 1980s, one organisation stood out as leading the promotion of health in Manchester's BME communities, and placing their needs on the health service agenda, both locally and nationally.

In 1986, the NWRHA issued guidelines to health authorities on how to implement strategies for "Better Health Care for Ethnic Minorities". But there was no prior consultation with the minority ethnic communities in Manchester, even with the large inner-city Caribbean population, which had been established since the 1950s. In response, the North West Association of Community Health Councils held a seminar, and much dissatisfaction was vented, both with the guidelines and their preparation. Following a series of community-based meetings, and with assistance from the Central Manchester Community Health Council (led by Nick Harris) and from some local elected representatives, Manchester Action Committee on Health Care for Ethnic Minorities (MACHEM) was formed. As a voluntary organisation, its mission was to promote equity and eliminate discrimination, on the grounds of race or religion, in the fields of social care, health care, and community care, as well as employment in these areas.[42]

The origins of MACHEM, however, *can* be traced further back, to the late 1970s and early 1980s, when a group of ethnic minority health professionals formed an ethnic minority community health group. They had known discrimination, and set out to challenge what they saw as the ethnocentric way in which health care was delivered, and experienced, by both employees and the public. The group included Carol Baxter, a trained nurse and M.Sc. in Public Health at Manchester, who was then working at Manchester Health Education Unit. They received encouragement and support from individuals such as Judith Gray and Joyce Leeson, and from organisations such as the Commission for Racial Equality, and the Manchester Council for Community Relations. The group eventually faded, but as the events of 1986 demonstrated, the need remained, and Baxter was to become the Chair of MACHEM. As a former member of MACHEM pointed out, even the voluntary sector was Anglo-driven at this time, and the services they provided were often not culturally appropriate – for example, the 'meals on wheels service', whose meals did not match the dietary requirements of BME communities.

MACHEM worked to address the health needs of BME groups, and had some success with mental health, diabetes, catering, and facilities to meet religious requirements. MACHEM was essentially an umbrella organisation under which many BME groups shared common goals – which proved a strength, but also a source of problems. MACHEM's approach was informed by the community development model that was popular at the time. As a campaigning body, as opposed to a service delivery body, it supported and empowered organisations, as Carol Baxter explained, 'to negotiate, to engage, to address the issues, to look at issues'. MACHEM also facilitated the creation of groups, or 'front room ideas' as they called them, helping them to grow and ensuring that their policies were culturally appropriate. In this sense, MACHEM was a 'unique' organisation, but it was also something that people found hard to understand.

The focus of MACHEM's early co-operation with authorities in Manchester was the City Council, as they gave out the largest money grants. In the 1990s, however, MACHEM had to respond to changes in policy when the Community Care Act (1990) moved them from a grant system to contracts. Groups with a campaigning

Afro-Caribbean woman at a health event in Hulme, 2004.

COURTESY OF MANCHESTER PUBLIC HEALTH DEVELOPMENT SERVICE.

function would no longer have access to resources in the same way, and this placed more pressure on the voluntary sector to get their act together: as Baxter recalled, 'they needed to be stronger managed, have stronger management functions and a stronger track record in doing all sorts and compete a bit more vigorously for funding'. MACHEM succeeded in winning a contract of £0.75m to set up and manage a Princess Trust Carer Centre in the city. MACHEM was also heavily supportive of the establishment of counselling services at the Sickle Cell and Thalassaemia Clinic in Manchester, and orchestrated awareness-raising talks and seminars within the Asian community.

MACHEM folded in the 1990s, for complicated reasons. Its members were activists who gave up a lot of their free-time to the cause; long serving volunteers understandably grew tired of this very demanding work, and they had other commitments which crowded MACHEM out of their schedules. In the Blairite world of third sector provision, where charities were expected to behave like businesses and compete for contracts, MACHEM had trouble adapting. In representing a wide range of groups and interests, MACHEM had meant 'all things to all people'; it could neither articulate its existence nor modernise.

But it had already achieved many of its goals. MACHEM enabled a number of BME groups to get stronger so as to secure their own resources. Furthermore, many of those involved in MACHEM took their expertise, confidence and skills forward into other roles within the health service, at both the local and national levels, and as non-executive directors on health authority boards. It helped empower BME healthcare professionals, providing a channel through which they could address issues which the mainstream services would not allow them to address. MACHEM raised awareness of ethnic minority communities and jolted Social Services, the Town Hall, and the Health Authorities, into action.

The University in the Era of Community Medicine

The Department of Social and Preventive Medicine did what it could towards training staff for the new specialty of Community Medicine. Prior to the re-organisation, Manchester had replaced the Diploma in Public Health with the M.Sc., and had begun to offer a programme which paralleled clinical training, with registrar posts, in preparation for consultant appointments. Manchester graduates were thereby well placed to obtain membership of the Faculty of Community Medicine, founded in 1972, which required examination in the quantitative sciences, the behavioural sciences, genetic and environmental (including micro-biological) factors in health and disease, and health services organisation, followed by a posting at senior registrar grade, and a dissertation. Manchester was also one of the largest schools outside London providing refresher courses for MOsH making the transition to the NHS. The Department also changed its name to Community Medicine.

The Head of the department, Alwyn Smith, was elected to the Faculty of Community Medicine Board in 1972, and in 1981 became its President, serving nearly two terms in office. Locally, Smith addressed the inaugural meeting of the Manchester Medical Society Section of Community Medicine in October 1976, with a talk entitled 'Putting Community Medicine on the Map'. The Section gave local expression to the recent recognition of community medicine as a specialty in its own right. It was open to all doctors, especially those working in community medicine and community health, provided their qualifications were acceptable to the Council. Since 1875, the North Western Branch of the Society of Medical Officers of Health had held regular meetings. The new section of the Medical Society built upon this tradition, holding monthly meetings between October and May, at which an invited speaker would address a topical issue in community medicine practice or research. One session a year was devoted to papers delivered by recent graduates of the Masters in Community Medicine.

But in September 1978, Smith left to become Professor and Head of the newly created Unit of Social Oncology and Epidemiology (a combination of the Social Research Unit and the Regional Cancer Epidemiology Unit), based at the Christie Hospital.[43] He wanted to return to research, having, in his own words, 'become more of an educator than a research worker'. In a rather curious role swap, Ian Leck, a Reader in Community Medicine at Manchester and Honorary Medical Director of the Regional Cancer Epidemiology Unit was recruited as Smith's successor in 1979. Leck had always considered himself an epidemiologist rather than a public health doctor. Another former student of Thomas McKeown, Leck had worked on the epidemiology of birth malformation and had held lectureships at Birmingham and University College Hospitals before being appointed to the Christie. Joyce Leeson had wanted the Manchester chair; it was at this time that she left to begin the NHS work we have outlined above.

The new Department of Community Medicine had much to boast about. With the establishment of the M.Sc. in Community Medicine, the degree in Nursing, and the M.Sc. in Health Education and Health Promotion, it had 'emerged as the most broadly based and forward looking of such departments based in a medical school in the UK'.[44] Its teaching and research covered not only epidemiology, but social and behavioural sciences, and statistics.

By 1978, however, leaders were less optimistic, and wondering how to respond to the manifest inability of the re-organised NHS to meet the challenges of public health:

> Integration of the services should have enhanced the potential to promote the health of our communities, and the allocation of resources was obviously one of the means for achieving this. Unfortunately these changes have coincided with severe resource constraints, so that the increasing emphasis on allocation has become the handmaiden of economy rather than of extended health promotion. The uncertainties have affected community physicians in particular, and many individuals have found themselves called upon to undertake new responsibilities for which their training has not always adequately prepared them.[45]

The Departmental Board placed its faith in a continued programme of undergraduate and postgraduate education and training, to meet the needs of community medicine practitioners. This did not, however, go far enough for Anthony Lane, Regional Medical Officer, who wrote to the Board concerned by the 'tragic separation of academic community medicine from the service field'.[46] The academic community, Lane argued, all too often overlooked that aspect of Community Medicine that promoted health through the planning of services, the deployment of resources, the study of relative priorities of community health needs in relation to the feasibility of intervention, the efficiency and efficacy of services, and the management sciences applied to health services. 'The Health Service in this Region', Lane continued, 'very badly needs such an academic approach'.

The 1980s brought no resolution, though the Department was still the region's leading training institution. By the start of the decade, the M.Sc. in Community Medicine had been opened up to non-medics, with places funded by the Health Education Council (HEC). Graduating at the time of another NHS re-organisation, the non-medics had little difficulty finding full time health promotion posts in the North West. With support from Robert Boyd, Professor of Child Health, Leck also succeeded in getting 'medicine in the community' added to the fourth year medical undergraduate curriculum. Alongside the traditional modules of medicine, surgery, paediatrics, psychiatry and obstetrics, students now spent some of their time attached to a general practice, and a local public health department.

The department was not much affected by the University's culling of staff, as a result of the Higher Education funding cuts announced in 1981. By 1984, the department had a reasonably large staff body. In addition to Leck, Leo Baric, Reader in Health Education, and Senior Lecturers, Tom Fryers and Joan Munro, the department had three Senior Lecturers in Computational Methods in Medical Science, four Lecturers, one Lecturer in Health Economics, two Lecturers in Health Education, together with many associates, including Judith Gray and Joyce Leeson. When Professor Tim Lee retired as Head of Occupational Health, Community Medicine was given responsibility for his staff, until the funding for a replacement Chair was raised.

However, aside from education and training, the department was not much involved with the health services research and planning that was supposed to be central to the community physician role. Earlier, Smith had reversed Brockington's policy of appointing lecturers with joint appointments to the local health authority; to some eyes this potentially distanced academics from what was going on locally – hence Lane's complaints.[47] Meanwhile, few of the new health authorities seemed interested in collaboration, especially those in Manchester. Tom Fryers worked with Salford, continuing the mental health work begun in the 1950s under Susser. Joan Munro (who was responsible for the social science input to the then 'preclinical' curriculum) was also linked to Salford, as a Specialist in Community Medicine (Social Services). Lecturer David Baxter spent several sessions a week as a Consultant in Community Medicine (Environmental Health) in Stockport. Only Selwyn St Leger worked as a specialist in Community Medicine in Manchester.

According to Leck, the department's research agenda was not much influenced by the demands of locality or region. This contrasts with developments elsewhere in the medical school, where several growing strengths were 'as much social as scientific'.[48] In geriatric medicine, the new Diabetes Centre, and the Arthritis Research Campaign (ARC) Epidemiology Unit, for example, the University made major contributions to shaping local health services.

Overview

This chapter on the history of public health within a re-organised NHS has again presented an accumulation of new concerns, from health promotion to the new public health, from the exposure of health inequalities to the resurgence of communicable disease. Public health became progressively more sophisticated in its target groups, e.g. women and black and minority ethnic communities; it also became increasingly concerned with lifestyle, focusing on single issues related to chronic diseases, such as smoking and lung cancer.

Figure 4.1   Standardised mortality ratios, all causes of death, Manchester,
Salford, Stockport, Liverpool, and Birmingham Local Authorities, 1974–1990.

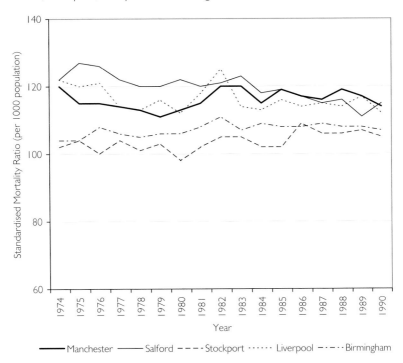

Source: Local Authority Vital Statistics, Series VS no.1 1974–no.17 1990.

Historians exploring this period in the national history of public health have described a decline, starting with the NHS re-organisation in 1974, and ending with the Acheson Report in 1988, which marked a 'new beginning' for public health. We too have mapped organisational problems and disorientation in the NHS, and a progressive lack of innovation in the University. But North Manchester was a 'beacon' in terms of its health initiatives, although its impact in terms of health improvements is more doubtful, and the City Council fought for a role in the broader public health agenda at a time when this was largely denied by central government. The city's leaders rose to the challenge of the Black Report, despite government misgivings; and despite early panic, they dealt competently with the advent of HIV/AIDS.

As a specialism, public health in Manchester did suffer, professionally and organisationally, from its position within a re-organised NHS, but the local championing of health and health services was alive and well, in some areas at least. Yet, by the beginning of the 1990s, Manchester still compared poorly with other major English cities in terms of overall mortality, as figure 4.1 reveals.

CHAPTER FIVE

The 1990s: Public Health and Neo-Liberalism

T HE NEO-LIBERAL VISION of Britain had strengthened and deepened during the Thatcher years, and especially after her popular success in rescuing the Falkland Islands. Few Thatcherites liked the NHS – it seemed a bastion of union and professional power, and far too large. But they recognised its popularity and public suspicion of Tory intentions. The intellectual resolution of this dilemma came from American economics, which had expanded since the 1970s to explore market mechanisms in public services. If purchasing authorities could be separated from supplier authorities, then a quasi-market could be constructed.

Ken Clarke, as Health Secretary at the end of the eighties, rejected insurance models and settled for internal markets. Hospitals could be made financially autonomous, and health authorities could purchase their services. In addition, some 'fund-holding' GPs could purchase hospital services on behalf of their patients. The hospitals were expected to compete for patients. Health authorities would work with hospitals to plan services, and they would buy those services for which the money was not routed through GPs. They would also be responsible for public health functions – which were increasingly marginalised, except where they could be passed to GPs.

The market model never became dominant, and was attacked by Labour politicians as divisive and preventing proper co-ordination of services. The GPs who took advantage of the new arrangements enjoyed their new freedom to develop their practices, and without doubt the scheme did transfer some power away from hospitals. One concern was the advantages gained by fund-holding GPs and their patients, over those doctors who did not take part.

New Labour argued for the power to be transferred to local associations of GPs, and when Tony Blair won the election of 1997, the plan was to spread GP power, and to also make public health an end in itself. Hospitals were to be improved by target setting; they had financial responsibility but little real autonomy. This direction of travel lasted for about three years, for two of which expenditure was severely limited. But after the planned expenditure was radically raised around 2000 in a dash for growth, Blair rapidly became convinced that targets and planning with the professionals would not act quickly enough. The NHS was now a central concern of government, and the answer, it seemed, was to return to market mechanisms, and push them far beyond the Tory experiments, especially by paying private companies to compete for NHS funds. Confidence in the wisdom and power of Downing Street 'delivery', produced ever more frequent re-organisations, which demoralised many staff and wasted huge amounts of public money.

For public health workers, re-organisational problems were compounded because their work depended on population information and links with local government. When boundaries were changed or organisations re-configured, it was hard to restore the links and the working relationships. Each re-organisation cast long shadows back and forwards and in the worst periods there were no unshadowed spaces. If there were gains, they were largely in data gathering, using the rapid advances in information technologies.

Public Health in Rapidly Changing Contexts

The development of public health in Manchester in the 1990s can be divided into three phases. The first, from 1990 to 1994, witnessed the introduction of the internal market, and the announcement of the Conservative government's *Health of the Nation* strategy in 1991, which set targets for the reduction of illness and mortality. While these two changes had a number of negative effects on public health, they both required better information on health needs and outcomes, and led to more gathering of information. This in turn promoted a burgeoning of what is referred to as 'multidisciplinary public health'.

By the end of the second phase, 1994 to 1997, public health staff in Manchester felt undermined and demoralised. Another re-organisation of the NHS in 1994, had further weakened a service already struggling with the fragmentation caused by the purchaser/provider split. The hospital agenda dominated the new Manchester Health Authority, and Manchester had no Director of Public Health between 1996 and 1998. Rationalisation of hospital services in the city caused political tension, and bad relations between local government and the NHS. At the same time, the re-structuring of the City Council in a bid to cut spending and rationalise operations, led to many statutory functions with a public health component being either abolished or dispersed among other departments, weakening local government's foothold in the broader public health/health inequality agenda.

The election of a New Labour government in 1997 ushered in an apparent resurgence in public health. In this third phase, prominence was given to prevention and health improvement in ameliorating health inequalities. The strategy was outlined in the white paper, *Saving Lives: Our Healthier Nation* (1999), the NHS Health Improvement Plan, and in the recommendations of the Second Acheson Report (1998). Local authorities were expected to work more closely with the NHS, and were given statutory powers to improve the well-being of their localities.

In 1997, Manchester was awarded 'Healthy City' status, and in 1998 it became one of the first Health Action Zones, in collaboration with Salford and Trafford. These local health strategies did produce some positive results, and helped to ease disagreements between the City Council and the NHS, though not without difficulties.

In the University, by contrast, a significant lull in public health activity was followed by an injection of new blood. But internal pressures related to funding, and research assessment, soon began to take their toll. At the end of the 1990s, the University of Manchester was without a professorial lead in Public Health, and the department's educational programme was under threat.

Research Informed Services and Multidisciplinary Public Health, 1990–1994

After 1991, health authorities became 'purchasers', whilst their previous 'provider' functions (responsibility for the management of hospitals, clinics and community services) were transferred to Hospital and Community Care Trusts. As 'champions of the people', health authorities were to identify the health needs of the local population and make contracts with service providers.

The changes were accompanied by some financial allocation, but limits were at first placed upon the choice of providers and the services bought were basically those currently being used. A decision was made in the North West region to implement block contracts to provide stability for hospitals at the time of the implementation of the internal market. This was a conscious attempt to ensure a smooth take off. In Manchester, a Joint Purchasing Unit, later renamed the Purchasing Consortium, was established to negotiate and monitor the contracts made with the management of hospitals, clinics and the voluntary sectors in all three Health Authority districts, enabling city wide expertise in purchasing to be built up at less cost.[1] However, with three districts to satisfy, the new scheme was complicated. As all three Health Authorities tried to turn their services into Trust services, there was considerable jostling for position at Board level. Reports of the period attest to an intensely political atmosphere, in which it was very hard to get agreement.

Public health considerations were deemed vital to the support of the commissioning process, and public health doctors from the three Health Authorities took greater roles in purchasing. But they worried about their ability to fulfil their other functions in such an environment. The cultural shift inevitably caused some disruption and conflict between different parts of the service, and diverted effort and money towards clinical provision, and away from activities such as health promotion and reducing inequalities.

The introduction of competition also appeared inconsistent with the government's new health strategy, *Health of the Nation*, which set targets for the reduction of mortality, and health improvement in five key areas of coronary heart disease and stroke, cancer, mental health, HIV/AIDS and sexual health, and accidents. In an article published in 1991, Joyce Leeson asked critically: 'Will it be possible to address inequalities by involving communities' intersectoral work, and ensuring the creation of quality services … just by setting contracts?'[2]

While multidisciplinarity had been a feature of the broader public health movement since its sanitary phase in the nineteenth century, as a professional occupation in the late twentieth century, public health was overwhelmingly dominated by medics.[3] But as NHS reform in the early 1990s demanded better health information systems, social scientists and researchers were increasingly drawn into the professional health services. Their services were necessary, but they enjoyed less pay and recognition than medics doing similar work.

Public Health Resource Centres (PHRCs) provide a good example of multidisciplinary public health in action, in and around Manchester. Between 1991 and 1994, five PHRCs were established across the North Western health region, initiated by the Regional MO/DPH Dr Stephen Horsley. These were Bolton, Wigan, Salford, Trafford (located in Salford); West Lancashire (located in Preston); East Lancashire (located in Nelson); West Pennine (located in Oldham); and Manchester. Funded partly by the region and partly by the health authorities, and staffed by a wide-range of social scientists, PHRCs provided statistical data, research capability, and public engagement skills necessary to actually *do* public health in the local area.

The Manchester PHRC assisted in the production of *Health Inequalities in the 1990s* (the follow-up to the 1986 report *Health Inequalities and Manchester*), and conducted the Manchester 'Baseline'

A community speaks out in Hulme. Central Manchester Health Authority, Report of the Director of Public Health, 1992. Produced with the help of North Manchester Medical Illustration Department. Research by Pius Nkamuhayo (Afri-Craft).

PHOTOGRAPHY BY LOUISE RHODES AND HARRIET THOMPSON

Health Needs Survey in 1992. It also assisted the public health departments of the three Health Authorities, in developing health needs assessments. A strategy was developed for Manchester setting out 'explicit values of equity, effectiveness, efficiency and promotion of health, well-being and autonomy of users'.[4]

With cost effectiveness a priority, purchasers had to improve their information gathering, so as to identify more closely with the resident populations. To aid commissioning, public health doctors in North Manchester analysed the social geography of the district using 1981 Census information. Rather than use electoral wards, which are designed to have equal numbers of people and often include both affluent and deprived areas, North Manchester was divided into twenty-four zones, each grouping enumeration districts with similar characteristics. Such zoning helped in deciding the positioning of new services.

In Central Manchester a system of 'rapid appraisal' was developed, which enabled the district public health team, under their DPH, Di Chisholm, to act on the recommendations of health needs assessment, and evaluate the effect of change. One such appraisal was carried out in collaboration with the Hulme Health Forum (HHF). HHF was set up in 1992, to share information about services with different sectors, to research health needs in the area, and to respond by altering services or developing new ones.[5] It was funded by small grants, with administration provided from the Single Regeneration Budget (SRB) to stimulate new projects on a wide range of topics, from oral health promotion to self-help groups.[6] The work paid off. In 1992–1993, Hulme Regeneration allocated £20,000 towards the work of the HHF. As a result of the rapid appraisal, a further

£40,000 was allocated to the priorities in the Action Plan devised for 1993–1994. Most money was allocated to schemes that prioritised joint-working and sought to reduce local health inequalities.

Thus, the broader public health agenda played a substantial role in re-developing Hulme. Public health efforts also tied in with the overall regeneration of the area that was being undertaken as part of the Hulme City Challenge initiative, an ambitious programme of inner-city regeneration, with three targets – housing, economic and social. The legacy of this work can be seen in the area which has changed greatly especially in terms of its architectural environment.

Public Health Under Attack, 1994–1997

In 1994, there was yet another re-organisation of the NHS. Nationally, the number of health authorities was reduced. In Manchester, the three health authorities merged to form a single Manchester Health Authority, with a number of detrimental effects on the status of public health in the city. The new Health Authority was preoccupied with sorting out strategic changes in the city, and highest priority was given to the rationalisation of hospital services, including the closure of inpatient and A&E services at Withington, the centralisation of neurosciences at Hope Hospital in Salford, and the plan for a new specialist children's centre in Central Manchester following public consultations. The sorting out of these tertiary services in Greater Manchester was seen by many as a necessary undertaking, but they did divert attention away from public health.

Manchester Health Authority's lack of interest in public health was epitomised by their failure to appoint a Director of Public Health between 1996 and 1998. Manchester lacked strong leadership in the specialty, although the Public Health Directorate of Manchester Health Authority maintained a lead team of three consultants and two specialists in public health, each of whom took an interest in one of the Authority's six localities for GP commissioning.[7] As one public health specialist, recalled: 'We learnt a lot through not having a public health director … we had to stand on our own two feet, and it was quite an interesting time'.

The re-organisation also had an impact on health intelligence in the city. At the same time that the Health Authorities merged, the North Western and Merseyside Regional Health Authorities came together to form the North West Regional Health Authority. There was a change in Regional DPH (John Ashton replacing Stephen Horsley) and with it a change in model for the public health information and intelligence function at the regional level. The region withdrew its funding of the PHRCs, and would later support the establishment of the North West Public Health Observatory funded by the Department of Health (based upon an earlier model established by Ashton in Liverpool). For a while, the PHRCs continued, the Manchester PHRC serving the newly merged Manchester Health Authority, but they did not survive the formation of Primary Care Trusts in 2002.

Alongside the disruption and uncertainty caused by the merger of three Health Authorities, funding was also an issue. NHS cuts announced in 1992, meant that Manchester was set to lose around five per cent of its funding over the next five years – at least £10m from Manchester as a whole. In 1996, Manchester was one of only two Health Authorities which did not receive growth money from the Department of Health. Funding cuts inevitably brought cut backs in public health, where management costs were high and personnel considered dispensable.

The re-organisation did finally bring the coterminosity between local authority and NHS boundaries, that so many in Manchester had long desired. However, longstanding disagreements between Manchester City Council and the local NHS, meant that it took a long time for alliances to be rebuilt. In the 1980s, the City Council had fought for a role in the wider public health agenda, at a time when the NHS did not systematically involve it in strategic decisions. Meanwhile, vehement protest over NHS reforms and the proposed cuts to local hospital services at Ancoats and Withington Hospitals in the early 1990s, had intensified political tensions between the two organisations. Distinct cultural differences, especially in terms of accountability and management style, also created difficulties for partnerships.[8]

The mid 1990s were also problematic for public health at the City Council. In 1996, council restructuring moved the corporate lead on health issues to Social Services, but the functions of the Environmental Health Department had already narrowed significantly. For a long time, local government's role in the broader public health agenda had been under attack, both from within and outside local government.

Around 1987, the Leftist administration of the City Council, under the leadership of Graham Stringer, as noted above, had embarked upon a more entrepreneurial approach. According to Steve Quilley, they subordinated socialist commitment and community development to the economic and global primacies of urban renewal; 'defending jobs, improving services' tended to become 'growth first, welfare later'.[9]

This new direction was exemplified by the Council's increasing co-operation with both central government and the local private sector, its embracing of redevelopment schemes such as City Challenge, City Pride, and Single Regeneration Budgets, much of which went into physically rebuilding parts of Manchester, and in its approach to the Olympic/Commonwealth Games bid process. One criticism of the early stages of the regeneration of Hulme, as mentioned earlier, was that it was much weaker in attending to the economic and social needs of the community than the environmental condition of the area. Strikingly, these interventions in urban renewal lagged behind, and contrasted with, those in cities such as Liverpool and Glasgow, where the large-scale cultural events of the National Garden Festivals in 1984 and 1988 had promoted health, well-being and the environment.

This was also a period of contraction in council services, as all city councils were required to reduce expenditure. Voluntary early retirement was introduced across the Council, and training budgets were gradually reduced to a minimum. In line with national trends, student Environmental Health Officers (EHOs), for instance, were moved to partial sponsoring, usually in the form of a bursary, and the provision of practical training during vacation time and for the compulsory third year. Certain functions and staff were also transferred to other departments, for example, EHOs and Technical Officers working on private-sector housing were transferred to the Housing Department.

Shifting national agendas further reduced the role of the Environmental Health Department in the early 1990s. The Audit Commission, undertaking a review of the Environmental Health Department as part of a national survey, concluded that some of the department's non-statutory functions were surplus to requirements. Home safety was one area that was criticised, and the dedicated unit was subsequently abandoned. Michael Eastwood, Director of Environmental Health, found it difficult to comprehend that actions that were designed to prevent injury or death, and were supported by their public health colleagues, were criticised in this way, especially when targets for accident prevention appeared in successive national plans, starting with *The Health of the Nation*.

More change came with the replacement of the post of MOEH with that of Consultant in Communicable Disease Control (CCDC), and its removal from the Local Authority to the Health Authority in 1992. This had been another recommendation of the Acheson Report (1988). This development, however, was welcomed in Manchester, where Eastwood was facing the prospect of reducing spending across all parts of his department. He felt that medical advice was needed more for communicable diseases than for environmental health issues, and that it would be better resourced and supported within an NHS public health department. The MOEH, Mike Painter, agreed. The public health departments eventually agreed to properly support the post, and an Infection Control and Surveillance Unit (ICSU) was set up, based in Darbishire House. The CCDC remained the proper officer of the Local Authority for communicable disease control, and EHOs were made available to assist in investigations.

A Renaissance in Public Health, 1997–2000

In 1997, a New Labour government introduced a revised national health strategy, set out in the white paper, *Saving Lives: Our Healthier Nation* (1999). The strategy reduced the number of national targets for reducing mortality and ill health to focus on heart disease and stroke, accidents, cancer, and suicide. *Our Healthier Nation* also placed greater emphasis on the building of partnerships between local government, the Health Authorities, communities, and voluntary organisations, for example in local Health Improvement Programmes.

By the mid 1990s, it was widely recognised that the health gaps between deprived areas and the country as a whole had widened. 'Health Action Zones' (HAZs), were meant to reduce health inequalities by focussing on areas of high need.

Under New Labour, local authorities were given a statutory duty to promote the well-being of their communities. Meanwhile, the 1998 Acheson Report into inequalities in health, had identified thirty-nine policy recommendations to tackle the social and economic determinants of health. Of these, only three specifically addressed the role of the NHS. The rest focused on broader social and economic determinants, which would require multi-agency responsibility.

Public health in Manchester was also reinvigorated in this period.[10] In 1998, a new Director of Public Health was appointed, Dr Ann Hoskins. More staff followed, and two local health programmes got underway at the end of the 1990s: Manchester Healthy City, and the Manchester, Salford and Trafford Health Action Zone.

Manchester Healthy City
Manchester officially launched its Healthy City initiative on 2 June 1997, at the Bridgewater Hall. The initiative was inspired by the WHO, and sought the 'concrete appeal and involvement of the public'.[11] It featured: political commitment; the consideration of health in relation to all policies and programmes; an emphasis on prevention and working across agencies; tackling the most urgent problems; and improving the health of those with the worst health.

Manchester Healthy City was jointly financed by Manchester

Health Authority and the City Council, although the money sat with the Health Authority. Securing Healthy City status was viewed as an attempt to make Health for All more of a corporate priority across the Council, and between the Council and the NHS. However, the initiative was not an immediate success; it remained very much on the margins. In the absence of a DPH, Manchester appointed a Healthy City Co-ordinator, Pam Ashton, based partly with the NHS at Gateway House, and partly with Social Services at the Town Hall. She was expected to deliver a very ambitious programme, against high and very different expectations, and she did not enjoy the support of Manchester Health Authority.

The Manchester Healthy City initiative brought greater strategic commitment from the City Council, and went some way towards mending relations between the health and local authorities. But it initially led to discontinuity in posts at the Council, some of which had been established in 1986. The Health Promotion Unit, for example, was disbanded, as posts in health inequalities and health development were replaced by jobs within the Healthy City initiative.

In 2000, the post of Healthy City Co-ordinator was moved entirely over to Social Services at the City Council, largely because the Local Authority was considered the better position from which to look at the wider determinants of health. It was also considered a more secure location, given the likelihood of another NHS re-organisation. The Healthy City project was then asked to take the lead on a teenage pregnancy programme and a mental health programme, both of which brought staff and resources. A team of five was quickly established, and some Health Action Zone (HAZ) money was obtained.

Manchester, Salford and Trafford Health Action Zone
In 1998, a local bid to become a HAZ, made up of Manchester, Salford and Trafford Health Authorities and the three Councils, was successful. The HAZ programme, introduced by the New Labour government, gave official emphasis to public health and health inequalities, and was intended to bring together organisations both within and outside the NHS, to develop and implement strategies for modernising services in areas of highest need.

Manchester, Salford and Trafford, came together in recognition of their shared deprivation. Fifty-one of the seventy-four wards in the HAZ had deprivation levels above the national average; although, in comparison with Manchester or Salford, Trafford had relatively few wards which had sufficiently high levels of deprivation to warrant HAZ money being spent in them. The main focus of the HAZ was

Table 5.1   Status of children living in households within the Manchester, Salford and Trafford Health Action Zone.

Children living in households …	Manchester, Salford and Trafford HAZ	England & Wales
with no earners	30.6%	17.2%
with a single parent	22.6%	13.2%
lacking/shared amenities (including no central heating)	15.6%	14.8%
with no carer	37.9%	21.0%

Source: Manchester Health Authority, Annual Public Health Report, 1997/98.

the problems facing children and young people, including sexual health, health issues among older people, and those of people with mental illness.

The simpler boundaries and less complex relationships no doubt facilitated joint-working. However, like the Healthy City Initiative, the HAZ was overstretched. Brought together simply in recognition of a shared inner area of deprivation, the HAZ was not a natural collaboration. The artificial boundaries across two health authorities and three local authorities created many different and competing tensions.

Changes in personnel and policy at the Department of Health also hampered progress, as one senior public health doctor reflected:

> … the problem with Health Action Zones is as soon as they were set up they were driven continually by different policies, so I mean they weren't really given the chance to embed, and every new Minister sent them on a slightly different direction … it went from being very loose to absolutely micro-management.

An evaluation of the Manchester, Salford and Trafford HAZ carried out by researchers at the University of Birmingham, also confirmed that by October 2000 National Health Service targets relating to performance management had reasserted themselves, marking a return to a medical model of health policy and reducing the local freedom and community development that the HAZ strategy had originally promised.[12]

Nevertheless, the HAZ had important successes, including the Wythenshawe Health Strategy, the emergency contraception scheme, and tobacco control work. The Wythenshawe scheme was a major investment with lasting effects in an area of high deprivation; it was more socially focused than most of the inner-city regeneration schemes. The implementation of emergency contraception in co-operation with Manchester pharmacists was also a success, although it was 'a battle against the tide'.

The HAZ also shifted the impetus of public health towards health inequalities and the determinants of health. As one informant commented, it brought 'new models of ways of working', especially with the communities of the HAZ, as well as 'new ways of engaging people and new solutions'. While some initiatives worked and others did not, 'it was a different way of saying how are we going to get into the most deprived areas?'

This cross-fertilisation of ideas was an important and lasting legacy of the HAZ, particularly ideas around social capital and social enterprise, arising from the work of researchers in Salford, such as Jennie Popay. Some of the Wythenshawe Health Strategy funds, for example, were used to conduct a feasibility study looking into developing a social enterprise that would fill some of the gaps in the care economy. In recent years, this has led to the establishment of 'Home Care Associates', through Manchester Enterprises – which should create more very local jobs for people in the care industry.

The University and the School of Epidemiology and Health Sciences

By the beginning of the 1990s, the Department of Community Medicine had become somewhat run-down and remote from local services. Leck retired as Head of Department in 1990. and as Professor of Community Medicine and Epidemiology in 1991. Stuart Donnan was appointed to a re-titled Chair of Epidemiology and Public Health, and as Head of Department. Donnan had been Foundation Professor at the new medical school in Hong Kong, where he had set up a thriving department of Primary Care and Public Health, and attracted research funding in excess of £350,000. Within a short time of his arrival in Manchester, the department was re-organised as part of a general restructuring of the medical school, becoming part of the School of Epidemiology and Health Sciences, which also included the ARC Epidemiology Research Unit. The use of 'epidemiology' in the new title was suggested by Donnan, who saw the two disciplines as separate, albeit overlapping. He thought it good that the University acknowledge epidemiology, although he was criticised by other academic heads for separating the science of public health from the interventions it served.

After Donnan's arrival, an injection of new blood seemed to reinvigorate the department. New appointments included the clinical epidemiologist, Kennedy Cruickshank, who was conducting important work on diabetes and ethnic minorities, and a Senior

Lecturer in clinical epidemiology and public health, who was a physician with a Ph.D. in medical informatics. (He was, unfortunately for the Department, head-hunted by a US-based company within six months of his appointment, which also precipitated the departure of the junior lecturer appointed at the same time.) Manchester remained an important centre of training in public health, feeding the local health service, and maintaining professional networks. The School also continued to focus heavily on its M.Sc. programme, which had changed to a modular degree prior to Donnan's arrival.

But for all his efforts, Donnan faced challenges from the outset. With the departure of Smith and Leck, and the subsequent re-organisation of the school, historical connections within the Manchester school of public health were inevitably lost, and relationships between the school and the other disciplines within the Faculty became strained. Although Donnan sought to strengthen connections with Occupational Health, and with those working at the Cancer Unit, he was up against strong personalities, and 'empire-building'. One historical collaboration which did survive was with Alan Silman and the ARC Epidemiology Research Unit, situated next door to Public Health. For a time, the two shared their research expertise, and participated in each other's teaching.

In 1988, the Acheson Report had recommended that academic public health be concentrated in a smaller number of specialist schools. Alwyn Smith and Stephen Horsley, then North West Regional DPH, had set up a small group to explore such a possibility. Members included Joyce Leeson; the Deputy Vice-Chancellor of Manchester Metropolitan University, Sandra Burslem; representatives from one or two health authorities in the region; the Pro Vice-Chancellor of Salford University, Edward Parker; and the Director of Environmental Health, Michael Eastwood.[13] A decision was finally made to support the formation of a Northern School of Public Health, with the then three Greater Manchester universities providing academic input to courses and seminars. A principal source of funding was provided by the Regional Health Authority, and the school was set up at the end of the decade, with a small office in Manchester Science Park. Although there were no plans to abolish the existing departments of public health, the initiative fitted with the policy of rationalisation and re-organisation in university structures instituted in the late 1980s, which had led in Manchester to the merger and abolition of some faculties, and the idea of creating super-schools in certain disciplines.[14]

Donnan was appointed Director of the Northern School of Public Health, and Michael Eastwood served as a part-time Director upon his retirement from the Environmental Health Department.

However, the school was beleaguered from its creation. Firstly, there appears to have been little funding from the start. Secondly, proposals for a collaborative Masters course created a conflict of interest for Donnan, since he was also supposed to ensure the survival of the Manchester M.Sc. programme and make it pay by attracting students. At this time, the number of trainees at Manchester was not rising, and by the late 1990s courses began to be cut or amalgamated, especially those which demanded time and money, such as health promotion. Finally, the venture was also felt to be of questionable value in light of the Higher Education Research Assessment Exercise (RAE): were the now competing universities to develop joint research programmes? The school folded after five years. Despite some collaboration and staff interchange, Donnan admits that 'the added value was hard to see'.

Although relations with the districts were generally good, Donnan found it difficult to work with the NHS at regional level because they had 'different time frames and attitudes' and 'different definitions of information.' As Donnan puts it, academic public health doctors were helping the health service 'indirectly' through research and teaching but it was 'at one and a half arm's length, not close up'. It was not always immediately obvious, he argues, what could be done that would be useful to the services. Soon after Donnan arrived, the department was asked by the Regional Health Authority to advise on resource allocation around the health authorities within the region. An exercise looking at health service utilisation was planned but in the end came to nothing.

The Manchester Medical Society's Public Health Forum also fell short of its potential. In the mid 1980s, concerns were raised by practitioners that not enough of the talks offered by the Section of Community Medicine were relevant to community medical officers. There were also calls to ensure that non-medics with an interest in community medicine were made more aware of the section, perhaps by changing the name of the section to include 'Community Health'.[15]

However the Section, like the Faculty of Community Medicine, appears to have been slow to recognise the trend. Up to the end of the 1990s, non-medics could only be honorary members of the Section, regardless of their achievements in public health. Meanwhile, council minutes record that in the 1990s, attendance at meetings of the Section remained 'small and select', despite attempts to attract audiences from a wide range of medical disciplines, and inviting Merseyside Directors of Public Health and academic leaders to both council and scientific meetings. Only in the late 1990s does the Section appear to have begun seriously discussing ways in which to promote itself among a wider range of public health constituencies.[16] A Chadwick Lecture was introduced in 1999, similar to the Duncan Lecture held in Liverpool, and intended to widen the audience. It was named for Edwin Chadwick, the Manchester-born 'briefless barrister' whose national enquiries had established 'public health' as a national concern in the mid nineteenth century.

Changes in higher education funding did not encourage local involvement; the RAE based funding largely on academic publications, and the more the School aimed for an international epidemiological research reputation, the less they were able to assist the local health services. In the event, they did well in the RAE of 1992 (scoring a 5 rating). In 1995, a National Primary Care Research and Development Centre was established at Manchester by the Department of Health, as part of a national competition, to undertake a programme of policy related research in primary care. Donnan recalls that the setting up of the centre courted disapproval among some of his academic colleagues in epidemiology, but he saw it as 'a very reasonable thing to do with public health money'. 'This to me', he argues, 'was part of the broad field of public health, the health service research side of public health'.

Donnan left his post in 1997 to work for the NHS in London, and a replacement was not appointed until 2000. Thus, just as public health was experiencing a resurgence in the NHS and the Local Authority, the University was without a professorial leader in the discipline. Before the end of the decade, a decision had even been taken to end the M.Sc., and so the survival of academic public health in Manchester looked seriously under threat.

Overview

With organisational change in the NHS, rationalisation of local government services, funding cuts, and successive national health strategies, the 1990s was a period of flux for public health. The introduction of an internal market to the NHS failed to take account of local differentials; the setting of national targets for mortality-reduction in clinical specialisms made it difficult to achieve improvements in health. Modernisation of the City Council in this period also proved counter-productive for reducing inequalities and improving the well-being of the population. Research as a basis for the development of services rose in importance, but the University contributed little of direct use.

Figure 5.1   Standardised mortality ratios, all causes of death, Manchester, Salford, Stockport, Liverpool, and Birmingham Local Authorities, 1990–2000.

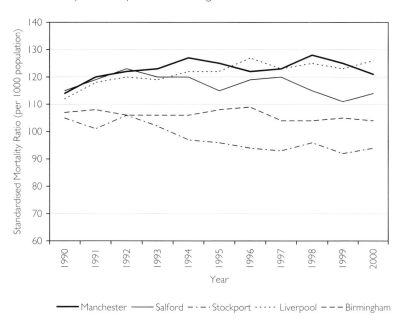

Source: Local Authority Vital Statistics, Series VS no.17 1990–no.27 2000.

On the plus-side, issues that had long been stressed at the local level, such as health inequalities, were finally legitimated in national health strategy. The relationship between the NHS and the Local Authority was being re-configured and, to some extent, improved in the latter half of the 1990s, with the Manchester Healthy City and the HAZ providing forums for collaboration. Allied to this was a more enduring concern with how the broader public health agenda could best be realised, a concern which would be carried through into the next decade. Specific programmes, such as the Health Action Zone, brought cash investment to the more disadvantaged areas of the City, leading to radical preventive measures, such as the provision of emergency contraception in a bid to tackle unwanted conceptions and teenage pregnancy, and thus aid the regeneration of depressed areas.

'Regeneration' characterised the style of public health adopted in this period; contrasting with the community-based, community-driven angle of the previous decade. Certainly, the 1990s witnessed an upturn in the fortunes of Manchester, with significant economic, social and environmental regeneration, involving local partnerships (private and public enterprises) and cross-department working. But there was little 'trickle out' from the city centre developments. Despite the cash-injections and the redeveloped housing, Manchester entered the new Millennium topping mortality tables and with most of its health gaps as wide as ever (see figure 5.1).

CHAPTER SIX

Public Health in the Twenty First Century

THIS BRIEF PENULTIMATE CHAPTER explores how city, health, and academic leaders in Manchester, have thus far responded to the challenges of delivering public health in the twenty first century. It picks up some of the abiding issues encountered in previous chapters: whether the function is currently best positioned to deliver public health; and the stresses and strains of re-organisation on professional morale and the delivery of services.

New Labour's bid to cut bureaucracy in order to save money continued into the new century. After what seemed a period of relative stability, the organisational structure of the NHS was once again re-configured. In 2002, Regional Health Authorities devolved into twenty-eight Strategic Health Authorities (SHAs), while Health Authorities gave way to new Primary Care Trusts (PCTs) via Primary Care Groups (PCGs) (see appendix 3), local commissioning bodies with responsibility for community-based health services. In Manchester, three PCTs were established covering North, Central and South Manchester, and placed under the authority of the Greater Manchester SHA. By July 2005, only three years after the last re-organisation, the government published its plans to make further significant changes to the structure of the NHS. This time, the number of PCTs and SHAs was reduced. In 2006, North, Central and South Manchester PCTs merged to form a single Manchester PCT, and the North West Regional Strategic Health Authority was created from the merger of the Greater Manchester, Cumbria and Lancashire, and Cheshire and Merseyside SHAs.

Compared with previous decades, the policy that accompanied New Labour's organisational changes in the 2000s, continued to give prominence to reducing health inequalities and improving population health. In *Shifting the Balance of Power* (2002), the government set out a new agenda which rooted public health at the centre of the new primary care organisations. PCTs were not only responsible for contracting with providers of secondary care, and managing GPs and primary health care, they were also to develop health promotion and address health inequalities. DsPH, from both medical and non-medical backgrounds, were to assume a strategic role in co-ordinating these activities.

Continued collaboration and partnership between the NHS and local authorities was another theme of this new agenda. Having already encouraged NHS and Local Authority agencies to work together on such things as HAZs and Health Improvement Plans, the Local Government Act 2000 made it the duty of local authorities to produce a community plan or strategy, that addressed the future social, economic and environmental well-being of their communities. In 2002, the new agenda allowed for joint DsPH appointments between PCTs and Local Authorities.

Between 2002 and 2006, a succession of policy changes and reports have further emphasised the importance of the public health function. In 2002, Sir Derek Wanless, a former Chief Executive of the National Westminster Bank, was asked by the Chancellor of the Exchequer to report on the resources which would be required, to ensure that the NHS could remain a publicly funded, comprehensive and high quality service. The Wanless Reports (published in 2002, and its follow-up in 2004) highlighted the impact that lifestyle changes might have on future NHS resource requirements, and the need to develop an evidence base on the cost-effectiveness of present and future interventions. *Choosing Health: Making Healthier Choices Easier* (2004), and its follow-up *Delivering Choosing Health* (2005), set further performance frameworks for all health and social care organisations, and local delivery targets focused on specific disadvantaged groups. But the focus of such reports and policies, and the resulting public health activities on the ground, returned the emphasis to the responsibilities of particular groups or individuals and their personal lifestyles, rather than on the structural causes of inequalities and their relationship to the widening wealth gap.

Recent Health Trends in Manchester

Since 2000, Manchester has made some progress in addressing the poor health of its population. Manchester is one of the government's Spearhead Local Authorities, of which there are seventy in total. In these areas, where the health record is poor, the government expects to see faster progress in addressing geographical inequalities in life expectancy, cancer, heart disease, stroke and related diseases, than the national average. Figures for 2003–2005 covering deaths from all causes showed that mortality was lower than predicted, and figure 6.1 shows deaths from all cancers and circulatory diseases have declined over the last decade.

Figure 6.1 Mortality from all cancers, circulatory diseases and respiratory diseases in persons under 75, Manchester Local Authority, 1995–1997 to 2003–2005.

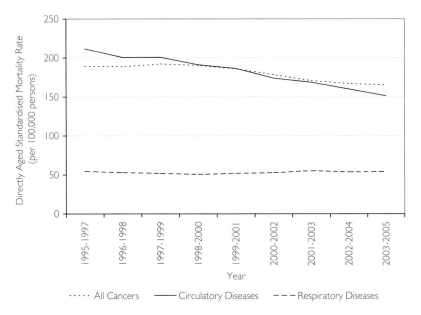

Source: Manchester Joint Health Unit, *A Picture of Progress: A compendium of statistics, 2007.*

Manchester is also set to deliver its contribution to the national health inequalities life expectancy target for 2010. Life expectancy is an important indicator of health inequalities, and table 6.1 shows the differences in life expectancy between males and females in Manchester, and between the three districts of the city. In 2003–2005, life expectancy at birth for men in Manchester was 72.5 years, while the average for England was 76.9 years. Among women, in the same period, life expectancy at birth was 78.3 years compared to an England average of 81.1 years. Male life expectancy in Manchester is the lowest in England, female life expectancy, the fourth lowest.[1]

Despite the progress, huge challenges remain to sustain the improvements, and to better tackle issues such as teenage pregnancy.

Table 6.1   Male and female life expectancy in years, 1993–2005 and for North, Central and South Manchester, 1993–2005.

3-year averages	Male	Female
1993–95	69.7	76.6
1994–96	70.0	76.9
1995–97	70.1	76.9
1996–98	70.4	76.9
1997–99	70.3	76.6
1998–2000	70.5	76.7
1999–2001	70.8	77.1
2000–2002	71.4	77.5
2001–2003	71.8	77.8
2002–2004	72.3	77.9
2003–2005	72.5	78.3
1993–2003		
Manchester	71.2	77.6
North Manchester	70.2	77.4
Central Manchester	70.6	77.2
South Manchester	72.9	78.2

Source: Manchester Joint Health Unit, *A Picture of Progress: A compendium of statistics,* *2007.*

Public Health in Primary Care Trusts

A public health directorate was established in each of Manchester's three PCTs. As the challenge around resources and relationships with the Acute Trusts became apparent, public health gradually made its way up PCT agendas. Prevention was to be employed to stem the flow of resources towards the local Acute Trust. In 2002, DsPH were given executive positions on the PCT Boards, and the posts were opened up to candidates from a variety of non-medical backgrounds – recognition that the strategic role they were to assume would depend less on medical qualifications, and more on leadership and political skills. The appointment of DsPH from outside medicine was popular in the North West, and Manchester appointed a number of such posts in 2002.[2]

The challenge for the Manchester PCTs was to deliver change locally whilst ensuring the integrity of a city-wide agenda. The three PCT Public Health Directorates worked together on public health targets around the issues of smoking cessation, immunisation, teenage pregnancy, and binge drinking. It proved much harder to implement agreed strategy at individual PCT level, where there were always competing tensions for resources. While some viewed the small footprint of PCTs as ideal for changing poor practices and for seeing what was being delivered at the local level, others would later argue that they were not effective.

Community Health Councils (CHCs) in England, long considered the 'voice of the people', were abolished by the government on 1 December 2003. Patient and Public Involvement Forums were eventually set up as supposed successors to CHCs, but already clear differences had emerged in how each PCT fed into their local communities and remained accountable. In Central Manchester, for instance, five Local Area Groups (LAGs) were incorporated into the structure of the PCT, to engage local people in the work of the organisation. Each LAG covered two or three electoral wards with around twelve members, including senior PCT staff, local councillors, a director from the Central Manchester Acute Trust, front-line health care staff and local residents. The LAGs met once a month and contributed to the organisation, development and commissioning of health services in the local area, in health improvement initiatives, and in raising the profile of the work of the PCT. North and South Manchester PCTs established similar local area, multi-agency working groups, but these tended to report back to the public via established forums, such as Healthy Living Networks.

In October 2006, the three Manchester PCTs merged to form Manchester PCT. Its Chair, Evelyn Asante-Mensah, believes that this larger organisation will remain connected to the localities of Manchester whilst addressing health on a city-wide basis. Building upon their good relationship with the Local Authority, the PCT now shares a commissioning strategy with the Council, which looks not just at ill-health, but also health and well-being, and inequality. She recognises that the PCT must be careful not to get trapped in their ivory tower, and that they need to have a presence in the city, and to recognise its diversities, so that what works for Central may not work in the North or South.

Since the establishment of PCTs, many feel that relations between the City Council and the health service have improved, especially as the benefits of joint-working include better processes, service improvements and health outcomes. It is anticipated that the coterminosity between the two organisations that was re-instated in 2006 will continue to strengthen joint-working. From the perspective of the Local Authority, which has to deliver services to all Manchester residents, having other like-minded organisations is 'crucial to achieving things quickly and successfully'. A recent report by the Audit Commission confirms this. At the start of their investigations in 2005, the Commission found that the Greater Manchester conurbation had no shared vision of health inequalities, no shared actions to narrow the gap, and a lack of ownership in recognising the value of collaborative effort. However, by the time its final report was published in 2007, the Commission had noticed a 'marked difference' in Greater Manchester's position to work together on tackling health inequalities for the wider population.[3] There are of course those who still feel strongly that the health agenda is better served outside the NHS, and that the wider determinants of health and the reduction of inequalities, are best tackled within an elected government structure.

The Manchester Joint Health Unit

One prominent example of the improved co-operation between the NHS and the Local Authority can be seen in the creation of the Manchester Joint Health Unit. Before the publication of *Shifting the Balance of Power* (2002), there was considerable uncertainty in Manchester, as elsewhere in the country, as to where the public health function would sit. Concerned that the creation of three PCTs would mean the loss of some strategic focus and co-ordination around common public health agendas in Manchester, the City Council and Manchester Health Authority explored a proposal to establish a joint health unit in the city. In 2000, Professor David Hunter and Susan O'Toole of Durham University, were commissioned to conduct a feasibility study, and develop an outline of options.[4]

The study drew attention to the 'unacceptable' health gap in Manchester when compared to the rest of the country, and its relationship to poverty, and its associated economic and social causes, and consequences. It highlighted the City Council's under-developed role in the local health agenda, and the lack of corporate co-ordination and understanding of the connections between its various departments and duties, such as environment or housing, and health. Current attempts to address the health gap, such as the Council's Chief Officer's Group on Health and the HAZ, were seen as having had limited success.

Wide support for the principle of a joint unit was found among those consulted, and two organisational models were proposed. The 'traditional model' of bringing together all the bodies concerned was considered ill-suited to the maintenance of a broad strategic role, and the wielding of corporate influence in areas such as regeneration, leisure and education. The 'radical model', was of a small, flexible grouping with minimal bureaucracy, free to address the strategic remit of narrowing the health gap without being bogged down by operational responsibilities. It would maintain evidence-based action but also be a 'think tank' to challenge council departments and the NHS, and to keep health on the local agenda. Hunter and O'Toole challenged the City Council and the NHS to 'be brave' in making this 'exciting and innovative idea' a success in Manchester.

After a commitment to resource provision from the Healthy City fund, the City Council and the new PCTs, it was decided to go for the more radical, cross-cutting model of organisation, and the Manchester Joint Health Unit (JHU) was established in April 2002. The Director of the JHU, previous Healthy City Co-ordinator, David Regan, reports directly to the Deputy Chief Executive of the City Council. The post of director is Faculty of Public Health accredited, and has equivalent status to DsPH. The steering group comprises a PCT Chairs' representative and a PCT Chief Executive's representative, as well as the Deputy Chief Executive and the lead Councillor for Health. It reports to a joint forum, and the DPH and the Director of the JHU work closely together to maintain the links between the Local Authority and the NHS. Based in the Town Hall, as the 'fit strategic location to work across the city', the JHU is nonetheless owned and accountable to Manchester NHS, the City Council and the Joint Board. At its creation, the intelligence and research team from Manchester Health Authority was brought across, to avoid division and to ensure economies of scale.

While public health was eventually given a strategic and operational place in the new PCTs, the JHU forms an important part of the public health system in Manchester, especially in co-ordinating the efforts of all the various agencies. During its first five years, the JHU has taken the lead on several key public health priorities: smoke free Manchester; the promotion of healthy eating through the Manchester 'Food Futures' strategy; improving the quality of life for older people through the Valuing Older People initiative; teenage pregnancy; the building of new health facilities in regeneration areas; securing a fair share of NHS resources and accessibility of NHS jobs for Manchester residents; alcohol misuse; and the collation of health statistics.

The JHU has also played several strategic roles: in promoting physical activity, including a strategic funding bid leading to the establishment of the post of Strategic Health Manager within Manchester Leisure; supporting the Manchester Health Trainer Scheme; ensuring that the Local Improvement Finance Trust (LIFT) delivers on behalf of Manchester PCT and the City Council; and leading the Investment Strategy Sub-Group which works to ensure that resources allocated under the Local Area Agreement achieve maximum impact in addressing health inequalities.[5]

The University and the Evidence for Population Health Unit

In 2000, after a gap of three years, Dr Richard Heller, a clinical epidemi-ologist from the University of Newcastle, Australia, was appointed to a new Chair of Public Health. Heller's idea was to develop an evidence-base for population health, like those developed for clinical medicine in the 1990s. With funding for one research associate and two lecturers, an Evidence for Population Health Unit was established.

Heller's first task was to undertake research, and develop a methodology for measuring the population impact of interventions. This work resulted in the publication of research papers and a text-book on the subject. Heller also transformed the public health teaching programme at Manchester. The M.Sc. course had ceased to exist prior to his arrival, so with a clean slate, he created a new, fully on-line Master's course in Population Health Evidence. This was the first such course in the UK, and one of the first internationally. It was a great success, drawing in at least 100 new students each year, many from overseas, through which the course contributed to international health development. Heller negotiated a fees reduction for overseas students, on the basis that the course was on-line and had no capital costs (a move that was overturned following Heller's departure in 2006). He was also determined to have a public health input into the undergraduate medical curriculum. This had just been revised upon his arrival so it proved a difficult task.

Heller found Manchester an academically inhospitable environment. Although he was given money to support posts and to establish the course, he found that a number of his academic colleagues were not happy with the imposition. While there were one or two joint grant applications, there was little sense of collaboration, especially in teaching. Conversely, Heller found the NHS very welcoming, and

Staff of the Evidence for Population Health Unit.

COURTESY OF ALISON HAMILTON AND PROF. R. HELLER

particularly supportive of the new Masters course. He was made to feel part of the local public health community, collaborating with a number of groups in the co-supervision of students' work, and in the development of monthly 'public health grand rounds' where an academic service approach to a particular problem was discussed. He was less successful in gaining local acceptance of the 'evidence-based' approach. At the time of Heller's arrival, a programme of NHS Research and Development had just ended, and with public health working towards centrally driven targets, there was little demand for research which did not deliver immediate results. In the words of one public health doctor, 'policy doesn't allow you to wait'.

Following the collapse of the Northern School of Public Health, Heller attempted to establish a network of academic units of public health in the North West – a model based on his experience in Australia, where such academic units had worked together very productively. The venture got as far as a name, a website and newsletters, but eventually came to nothing. Once again, academic competitiveness proved to be a stumbling block, with the larger schools at Liverpool and Lancaster seemingly unwilling to co-operate in sharing courses and teaching on-line. Liverpool, incidentally, is to now offer its own online Masters in Public Health. Heller sees this as a missed opportunity to create a world class course drawing on the strengths of two big institutions.

Heller retired in 2006. There has, as yet, been no decision to renew the post of Professor of Public Health. The other posts previously held within the Unit have subsequently been taken over by the ARC Epidemiology unit, in what has essentially been described as 'an asset stripping exercise'. The M.Sc. runs under the new title of Masters of Public Health: The Evidence-Based Approach, from within the Primary Care Research and Development Centre.

The Impact of NHS Re-organisations

The most recent re-organisation epitomises many of the organisa-tional and operational problems faced in public health since 1974. The 'human' cost, in terms of job insecurity and staff morale has been great. Whenever a new organisation has formed, senior profes-sionals have had the unpleasant task of being re-interviewed for their jobs. While some re-organisations have increased the number of available positions, mergers have reduced the number of 'top' jobs to go around. Another criticism is that the roller-coaster of NHS re-organisations over the last ten or so years, has also led to a loss of expertise and corporate memory. Meanwhile, existing organisations are made to feel that they have somehow failed; their public health efforts and achievements swept aside by new organisations wishing to start afresh. This too has had a devastating effect upon staff morale.

From an operational perspective, the pace of change, especially in the last decade has created difficulties in the ability of DsPH to influence those around them and to produce change through partnership working. One previous DPH in the region reckoned that you need at least four years in one place to be able to operate effectively and for people to trust you. The continuity of staff, and stability of organisational structure are, as we have seen, important for productivity in public health.

Re-organisations pose a distraction to public health, reducing momentum and sucking energy that many feel would be better channelled towards improving health. From the perspective of those charged with delivering public health services on the ground, re-organisations are difficult, confusing and frustrating periods. One health visitor we interviewed thought periods of re-organisation 'an absolute nightmare', with management unavailable, and new projects unable to get underway. There is also a danger that long-running operations might die out under a new organisation. A prominent example of this is the recent running-down of the Well Woman scheme in Newton Heath, North Manchester.

The changes which have occurred within health visiting, a core public health service, show very well the impact of NHS re-organisations. Before 1974, health visitors played a key role in infant welfare, antenatal care, tuberculosis prevention, infant life protection, and school health. Health visitors liaised closely with social workers and other nursing staff at the Town Hall. In overseeing entire families in their care, health visitors were aware of the particular problems within any given community. By the late 1960s, when health visitors had also begun liaising with GPs and hospitals, they were in a unique position to learn more immediately of those in need of help and assistance, providing a link between the MOH and primary care.

At the 1974 re-organisation, health visiting was moved out of the Town Hall and into the NHS. According to Cecilia Maxwell Bradley, Superintendent Health Visitor (1964–1974) and the first Area Nurse (Child Health) for Manchester (1974–1982), the re-organisation had a dramatic effect on her profession. They moved away from their colleagues in social work and welfare, and there was much anxiety at the time about the effect this would have on the people of Manchester.

Under the re-organised system, health visitors more or less continued in their traditional duties around infants, mothers and child protection, usually based within the city's health centres, alongside district nurses and school nurses. As before, the work involved a lot of advocacy on behalf of patients, helping people access the available services. However, Maxwell Bradley recalls that among hospital staff, many of those who got the chief officer posts 'had no clue as to community services', whilst school nurses and health visitors were still very much unaccustomed to working together, even though they often worked from the same building.

Some attempts were made to address such problems in the early 1980s. In South Manchester, for instance, an effort was made to forge teams within the localities, rather than having cross district strata dealing with the same families. The District Management Team tried to integrate the school health, health visiting, and maternal and child welfare services, making sure each had an appreciation and interest in the others' work. They also tried to get more health promotion in, alongside the 'weigh 'em and measure 'em' approach, getting the services to 'see themselves as health institutions rather than small mechanical facilities'.[6]

The emergence of health promotion and the 'new public health' in the 1980s presented health visitors with new opportunities. Merryn Cooke, who qualified as a health visitor in the mid 1980s, working first in Newton Heath in North Manchester and later in Moss Side in Central Manchester, remembers that at the beginning of her career she was able to do a lot of public health work, especially around the elderly, with things such as exercise and relaxation classes, health for the over-60s, health days, and liaising with chiropody (see section on North Manchester above).

With successive re-organisations of the NHS in the 1990s these opportunities faded. Health visitor caseloads were at first geographical, meaning they were able to do a lot with health profiles and the health data for a specific population. Later, the attachment to GP surgeries had both positive and negative impacts. Cooke found that liaison with GPs improved, and some good training was provided in a bid to improve teamwork and get GPs to listen to nursing staff. However, attachment to surgeries ultimately created more work for health visitors as not all patients lived in the district within which the surgery was based. Over time, it became increasingly difficult for health visitors, to justify why they were working where they were, and with whom. The recent shift to corporate caseloads has meant that a group of health visitors are now responsible for a particular population, a model incompatible with falling staff levels and training cuts in the profession. Meanwhile, the popularity of child protection work, and the expansion of new government schemes such as Sure Start, continue to alter the traditional terrain of health visiting.

But how does Manchester's experience of organisational change compare with the rest of the country? Would things have been any different had Manchester not undergone so much organisational change in such a short period of time? A comparison with neighbouring Stockport can provide some insight here. In Stockport, Stephen Watkins has enjoyed a long tenure as DPH. Since his appointment in 1990, Stockport has resisted merger and remained coterminous with the Local Authority. Watkins has promoted a 'working together' model in the face of Regional demands to merge and re-organise.

Refusal to merge has had its drawbacks, including the threat of complacency. But the existence of shared boundaries with the Local Authority has meant that there has always been a structure for promoting health matters in Stockport, whether formally, through the Council's Public Health Partnership Board, which provides response to the Annual Public Health Report, or informally, through close working-relationships and networks among long-serving staff.[7]

Unlike Manchester, Stockport has pursued a coherent public health strategy over an extended period. The Stockport public health team, in collaboration with the Local Authority, have been able to successfully pursue programmes, such as screening for Coronary Heart Disease or community development. Health Visitor Teams have been successfully established which include at least one public health worker. As figure 6.2 shows, Stockport has witnessed results in terms of improved health, which 'has moved from being slightly worse than national average to slightly better than national average'. Lessons might therefore be learnt, as Manchester settles into its third major NHS re-organisation in twelve years.

Figure 6.2   Standardised mortality ratios, all causes of death, Manchester, and Stockport Local Authorities, 1974–2006.

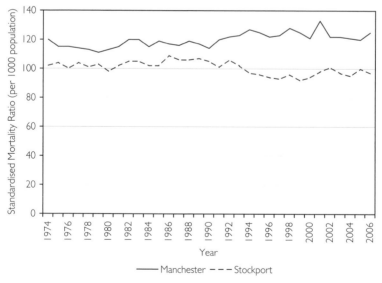

Source: Local Authority Vital Statistics, Series VS no.1 1974–no.32 2006.

CHAPTER SEVEN

Learning from History

I T IS NOT THE JOB OF HISTORIANS to prescribe for the future, or even for the present; but perhaps history is too important to be stuck in the past. We can at least hope to see our present as one scene in a long drama, as one configuration among many; and to learn thereby about what is specific to our time and our likely future; about aspects which may be seen as more or less perpetual; and about the middle ground – the problems which recur in new forms with new ages. This has been our approach. Here we indicate some of our findings, and add some suggestions.

Suppose we start where we began our chronology, with the Manchester of 1780 – a mercantile town on the brink of a rapid industrialisation which made world history. That was when local concern with public health began, with worries about rapid immigration, overcrowding, poor ventilation, and more generally about the failure of wealth to circulate adequately. The contrast between the luxuriously rich and the congested poor was already offensive. There are aspects of that Manchester with us still, both here and across the globe. In the shanty towns of most large cities one sees the problem hugely magnified. Across South and Central America, and much of Asia and Africa, that appalling contrast between rich and poor measures itself in millions of lives, where in Manchester it was tens of thousands.

Manchester's initial response was largely voluntary rather than statutory, and strong enough that Manchester Infirmary entered the global history of medicine for the foundation of a fever hospital, for public health regulations, and then for a kind of medical ethics.[1] This tradition of voluntarism – of collective action outside both markets and governments – has been one of Britain's political gifts to the world; it was central to public health efforts thereafter, and remains a key aspect of health politics (and healthy politics) now. But it proved insufficient as a counter to the negative consequences of rapid urban growth – as it still does across much of the globe.

In the classic period of industrial Manchester, the problems of urban immiseration became refracted into a discourse about place and dirt. A critique of filthy places overlaid the older economic concerns, and the answer was said to be clean water and the efficient removal of excrement.[2] And as with all such technical fixes, there were many critics who mocked the simplicities and looked to wider causes. Yet political and technical focus paid off, albeit slowly. The campaign took off in the 1830s, and by the 1860s municipal action overseen by central government had provided a series of reservoirs in Longdendale. Sewage removal focussed on dry-carriage, which has often seemed an unfortunate diversion, but perhaps there is reason to believe now that the use of pure water for sewage removal will come to seem an extravagance akin to our exhausting fossil fuels.

By 1900, Manchester was moving towards water-carriage of sewage, using water from Thirlmere, and a huge municipal sewage work using the latest biotechnology. The engineering works of John Frederick La Trobe Bateman and his successors, and the local discovery of activated sludge technology, would feature in any global history which showed how urban environments could be made more sanitary than their rural counterparts; how the traditional scourges of towns and cities could be removed by clean water, effective sewerage, and properly supervised food supplies.

These preventatives have been built, often literally, into our urban environments. We take them and their maintenance for granted except when, as in Manchester after 1970, spasmodic failure of sewers began to undermine the streets, and the holes were measured in DDBs (the volume of a double-decker bus). But social preventives are in many ways harder to embed and maintain.

When from the 1890s, through to the Second World War, Britain felt challenged as a nation – economically, militarily and imperially – the new mechanisms for the pursuit of 'national efficiency' were mostly social. They included reliable pensions, antenatal and postnatal care, education for mothers, health visitors and district nurses, dinners and exercise at school, and new experiments in social housing. These efforts 'peaked' after the Second World War in a nation with a strong collective sense, where decent housing, environments and education were seen as the condition, not just of equality of opportunity, but of collective responsibility for the young and the old, the sick and the under-privileged.

Since the 1980s, however, both Britain and Manchester have become more polarised as well as richer. It is not clear that the poorer areas of the city now afford the education and recreational resources which all communities need. It *is* clear that they often lack some of the voluntary action and self-help functions which make for healthy communities. Mutual support throughout life is fundamental to health, as has been clear for a century. Building and maintaining social bonds may be harder than for water pipes and sewers, but just as essential.

Around 1900, it was international competition, plus the threat of labour politics, that induced governments to support measures which had been voluntary and local. A century later, 'national efficiency' seems less a matter of competitive power, than of how we can best spend national resources in pursuit of national health. If we are to get good outcomes from medical and related expenditure, then we need to reduce needless sickness that overloads the system and reduces the potential benefits to individuals. The concept of *competitive national efficiencies* can thus become *co-operative national efficiency* which was one of the leading themes of the New Public Health. Good welfare states increase the efficiency of overall medical expenditure, and reduce inequalities which are themselves socially damaging. In this respect, Britain's alliances with the social democracies of Northern Europe are a precious inheritance, and its recent dalliances with American market systems seem unwise. No system is less efficient overall than that in the US. In no advanced country are the poor treated worse, and in none are there greater pressures for expenditure on medical commodities of debatable or marginal utility.

But public health now has a new horizon and a new dimension for national and local efficiency. The new millennium has brought home the threat of global warming and the likely disturbances of weather patterns, sea levels and agriculture, including direct dangers to health. We are just beginning to learn new ways of accounting – for a healthy planet, not just for material accumulation. But if these are not to become yet another way of burdening the disadvantaged, so as to slightly unburden the hitherto profligate, they will require new forms of material and energy economy – to use less fuel, less water, less ground. These desiderata, of course, chime with the oldest themes of public (and private) health – moderation of intakes, exercise, and good diet. A century ago, Manchester was, in part, a capital of vegetarianism, temperance and active sport. It is now, in part, a 'leisure capital', which often means cheap food, excess drink and spectatorism. And so the challenge is now all the greater.

The perceived threats to the early industrial city were dirt and contagious disease, which were considerably diminished by 1900. By 1950, some thought that infectious diseases would be conquered by immunisation and antibiotics. But we are not now free of contagions; we have learned to our cost that microbes are resourceful, even in the face of techno-scientific medicine. Epidemic diseases continue to appear or recur, and some pose major threats to population health, or bring back Victorian worries about hospitals as places of infection rather than cure. Epidemic diseases still demand vigilance and effective knowledge of their histories (sadly lacking in the recent case of Foot and Mouth Disease). New versions of hospital infections bring strict cleanliness back into fashion (e.g. against MRSA). Other new (and old) diseases proliferate through sexual encounters, and here the problem of contagion often comes back to that of mutual respect. Venereal disease is here symptomatic both of ignorance of the need for protection, and/or carelessness, often related to drink.

But since the 1950s, the most pressing of the new medical problems has concerned *chronic* disease, especially in conjunction with technologies which can relieve the problems, but not remove them. That we can get replacements for our joints and lenses is a great blessing – a good use of resources to extend comfort and activity into old age. But fewer joint replacements would be needed if fewer people were overweight. And for some expensive and less generally successful technologies, such as kidney transplants, much of the need also arises from diet, for example, via type II diabetes. Expensive treatments for the growing incidence of alcoholic liver disease offer a further example which is now attracting attention. One comes back to the clear fact of medical economics – that provision for good health is relatively cheap (but hard to ensure), whilst bad health is a huge but compelling drain on resources. This applies to mental as much as to physical health, and to the many interactions.

Of course, we do not know how chronic disease can be entirely avoided, no matter how well behaved we are; and we will not save the nation's funds if we avoid a quick death and then die slowly and expensively later. But we will have longer and happier lives – after which we might be ready to make fewer medical demands when the end is obviously nigh.[3]

How then shall we rate the prospects for the health of Manchester now and its public health services? De-industrialisation and movement beyond city boundaries have lowered the population, leaving a relatively impoverished local authority. The centre is a national example of a post-industrial leisure capital – and that brings problems as well as excitement. Some suburbs are prosperous, but huge areas containing public housing remain relatively deprived. Raising the health of populations here will require continued high investment in education, and recreational facilities for all ages, new employment opportunities and new ways of recreating community spirit.

To some extent the problem of social inequality in Manchester, and in the north more generally, reflects England's growing geographical inequalities. Raising the general level of prosperity in the Manchester City region will require national policies to counteract the dominance of London in terms of investment and employment, probably including major relocations of public sector jobs. Manchester is in many ways a test case of national seriousness about regional development. It has huge strengths, including its higher education and research, as well as considerable problems. This combination of need and opportunity ought to be an index for major relocations of public spending.[4] It is noteworthy that the North West has been to the fore in assessing the likely health impacts of major new projects in the region[5]

Organising for the Future of Public Health

Faced with these continuing problems, what shall we say about the public health effort and mechanisms, as evidenced locally over the last sixty years? Two observations, at least, seem clear: the first relates expenditure to organisation, the other to the intellectual basis of health-service reform.

In the post-war history of Britain there have been two periods where health expenditure became a priority: from the early 1960s, and from the early 1990s, especially 2000–2006.[6] The first saw considerable expenditure on hospitals, building on the economic improvements of the 1950s. The second saw lots more rebuilding, plus large increases in current health expenses, especially since 2000. But the potential impact of the recent spending was reduced by increases in administrative costs (including repeated re-organisations), by major extra charges (and potential charges) on private contracts, and by wage increases which in some cases exceeded reasonable expectations. Widespread demoralisation was a common result of institutional instability and of distant, poorly targeted micro-management.

Since the 1990s, details of health policies have become extraordinarily centralised, driven by the political need to respond nationally, rather than locally or regionally, to media-driven anger over examples of poor care or alleged injustice from 'post-code prescribing'. That Downing Street assumed it could run the NHS will surely come to seem a political-pathology with few equals. And as we have seen, public health services were particularly disadvantaged because of their persistent low priority and their dependence on good working relations with other statutory authorities.

The second, related general point concerns the extraordinary contrast between the neglect of evidence, consent and staff welfare in NHS re-organisation, and the concurrent achievements in clinical service, where evidence, consent and patient satisfaction have become the norms. At a time when the practice of medicine is providing sophisticated models of cautious empiricism, it may seem extraordinary that health service policy has been so dogmatic and unempirical. Indeed, in some ways the recent handling of the NHS recalls the 'quackery' of medical practice in Georgian Britain. With simplistic economics as their 'theory', policy makers have repeatedly peddled untested remedies, rarely stopping to analyse the results.

It seems clear that the NHS needs stability, plus local, incremental innovations, with proper assessment, and then a sharing of best practice. It is not well fitted to be driven top-down, nor does this model produce acceptable results.

Part of the problem here is a mis-reading of history that is sometimes deliberate. The NHS began, not as a state corporation, but as a network of professionals using state funds.[7] It ran from 1948 to 1974 with little structural change, and with a lower level of resource than in comparable countries – and the standards of medicine were transformed for the better. If by the 1970s it was falling behind other countries in some respects, that was more a matter of resource than of organisation. There is every reason to believe that the same structures, or those of the late 1980s, could have delivered the *real* improvements attained since 1990 – given the same investment (or less). We have seen that in North Manchester, in the not-so-prosperous 1980s, a decent stability gave innovative doctors and other health-care professionals, an opportunity to create a beacon in a backwater. How much more could have been done over the next twenty years had not re-organisation become a full time occupation? How many useful initiatives, e.g. under Healthy Cities or Health Action Zones, were stifled because of the presumption that health services could be re-organised like plants on a patio, when in fact they require prudent gardening?

On the difficult question of how public health services are best structured, we must begin where we are and move slowly, carefully assessing potential losses as well as gains. In this study, we have seen notable examples of public health initiatives, under both local government and the NHS. Manchester City Council, and especially Salford, were sometimes outstanding in the twenty years after the Second World War. The main factor was the energy and imagination of the MOH, backed by councillors. That one municipal officer had such power was probably advantageous, especially when compared with the diffuse responsibilities and resources with which later community physicians had to work. In North Manchester, in the 1980s, a strong NHS team, again backed by the governing board, made good progress, though sometimes at odds with the City Council, especially over closures.

Perhaps the anatomy of authority is less important than certain general rules for functioning. Experience with Healthy Cities and

Health Action Zones showed the problems of working between authorities. Teams worked better when brought together and placed in one site, in this case under the City Council. Wherever the funding comes from, and wherever the staff, there is much to be said for teams working within a single organisational culture, with a common form of assessment, as the Joint Health Unit also seems to show. In fields as diffuse and complex as public health, there will always be many questions of boundaries and cross-linkages, but these seem to be answered better where teams are reasonably secure and autonomous, rather than perpetually worried about re-organisations at various levels. Here there is some evidence that health professionals, such as nurses, tend to be more autonomous than local authority staff, for example social workers, but this need not always be the case. They are also generally better at disseminating information through professional (as well as institutional) networks.

In as much as good information-flows are required for collaboration, as well as innovation, and seeking information is generally more effective than being deluged, public health teams might have members assigned to know about neighbouring work, and about precedents and best practice elsewhere. Strong centres for the collection of local and regional data are also necessary, and these can benefit from long-term foundations, and close association with other social science disciplines, as well as a range of medical and related training programmes. In such ways we might build for a new age the regional responsibilities and competences which, in the years around the Second World War, were part of the global reputation of the University of Manchester.

That same period might also remind us of the powers over health which were held by local authorities before 1948, and of the activism of many city councils in developing those responsibilities in association with local professionals. The recent moves to bring NHS PCTs into closer association with local authorities, which seem to be working for public health services, may point the way towards wider collaborations around health and social services. This connection with local democracy, seems more convincing than the recruitment of volunteers to the boards of hospital trusts, etc., and it might also help increase interest in local government.

As we noted in the first chapter, one of the wartime arguments against depriving local authorities of their major health responsibilities, was the likely lowering of public interest in local politics. Local interest did indeed decrease and the recent extraordinary focussing of health politics almost exclusively on Downing Street might in some ways be regarded as a consequent problem.[8] Annual public reports on public health used to be a major way of focussing local attention (and spurring local rivalries). The Wanless Report called for their reintroduction,[9] and there would seem to be scope for connecting them with other reports on the city – partly to counteract the increasing paucity of quality journalism at local and regional levels.

Linking the PCT with the City Council could be one way of reducing the democratic deficit. Another, which may be complementary, is the recreation of CHCs which seem to have been the most effective 'voice of the people' in the recent history of the NHS, not least through their articulation with ethnic minorities. They seem to be the only recent NHS body whose death is commonly attributed to their effectiveness! Their resurrection might also offer a means by which more specific councils (for particular districts, community groups or services) might secure a public hearing. We can point here to the important roles of Manchester's black and minority ethnic representatives.

Some of the North Manchester experience may also be relevant here, as indeed are the longer histories. We know that health services, from late Victorian hospitals through to AIDS or cancer research, can be major agents of community cohesion as well as improvement. This integrative role of health services deserves more consideration now that social cohesion is high on the political agenda. It also needs to be considered when the geography of services is changed, whether as a result of 'rationalisation', or potentially as a result of individual 'choices' which may increase social stratification (as sometimes in secondary education). As we have seen, merging authorities and services in pursuit of marginal economies may substantially reduce community involvement, as well as the local knowledge and local commitment of staff.

Of course, such suggestions follow from a model of public life and health which includes collective action and strong political representation. These aspirations tend presently to be overshadowed by public discourse and policies which are grounded on economics rather than the careful development of services, on individual choices rather than representation and input, and on health services as commodities rather than as shared benefits.

Markets, Hierarchies and Public Health

As we conclude this book, one of the devices being touted by government is a variant of the voucher principle, which its members argued against in the 1980s – that social service users, and increasingly, health-service users, should be allotted funds which they can spend as they wish on their choice of services, from whatever providers.

Much effort is going into persuading employees and wider publics to support this plan, but relatively little into providing evidence that it will be effective. The potential gains to some groups may be clear, but the problems are also obvious – from assuring the quality and reliability of service providers, to ensuring the competence of user-choices. Will we secure yet more bureaucratic posts, as service-guides are added to assessors and providers, and how would the three roles be continuously co-ordinated, if they are no longer embodied in professionals trusted to balance need and resource? Can one hear the scandals coming over the horizon, with the calls for the reintegration of functions?

Such measures demand very careful and critical testing, on the basis of incremental change and attention to history. We have some relevant present models from the provision of residential and nursing homes, where choice is free and standards often appalling. Historically, it was to prevent the exploitation of the vulnerable by a combination of the greedy and the underpaid, that public authorities took over the business of mental asylums. The subsequent record was far from perfect, but a return to market relations offers little comfort, unless there is powerful regulation to enforce high standards, and sufficient resources to provide well for the needy. Otherwise, we go on sliding towards a means-tested health service, as in English dentistry, and as in countries, such as France, with social insurance systems.

By all means ensure that market services are available to the relatively poor in ways that may increase health – for example, through commercial gymnasia and health clubs. Supermarkets, which together have the privilege of supplying most of the nation's food, might do so in ways which clearly indicate its nutritional quality; they could at least meet the requirements of the government's 'traffic light' labels, and not persist with 'information' meant not to inform. They could also be more active in promoting healthy diets and local sources; perhaps such work could be a requirement of their planning permissions? In such ways, corporate responsibility to health policies could be profitably linked with responsibility to environmental policies, at local as well as national levels. Private and public corporations, including NHS agencies, should also be involved as employers, and not just at the level of stress counselling.[10]

Health is not just an individual commodity, whether purchased directly or through the state, and the issues around marketisation are peculiarly important for public health. There are now many agencies, both commercial and governmental, anxious to marketise services, and relatively few who will point to the role of mutualism and communal support in these areas. The collectivity of public services, and the involvement of users in their planning and operation, provide a vital complement to private actions and purchases, especially in districts where purchasing power is relatively low.

Social health may be as 'contagious' as social pathologies. For public health as for the environment, we all stand to gain from communities which, by acting together, can reduce harm and increase well-being.

Universities and their Roles

We have seen that Manchester University was outstanding after the Second World War in its innovative attention to public services. The decline of Public Health as a university discipline has removed the obvious focus for questions of population health and of associated services. It has also weakened the public health element in medical studies, as we noted for postgraduate courses. But at undergraduate level also, social issues tend to be marginalised.

The decline in academic public health in Manchester contrasts significantly with the apparent success of other departments in the UK such as the School of Population, Community and Behavioural Science at Liverpool, the Centre for Public Health at Liverpool John Moores, the Centre for International Public Health Policy at Edinburgh, the London School of Hygiene and Tropical Medicine, and the Department of Social Medicine at Bristol. Academic public health at the Liverpool Universities flourished in the 1990s, and the University of Liverpool hosted the original Liverpool Public Health Observatory, used as the model for the national scheme. More recently, the Centre for Public Health at John Moores University has hosted the North West Public Health Observatory. Both sites benefited greatly from the ideas of Dr John Ashton. At Edinburgh, the multi-disciplinary, social science, 'real world' approach, first established in the 1960s, has continued to be a prominent feature of both undergraduate and postgraduate teaching and research.[11]

Manchester University, especially around the Second World War, also played a key role in mediating between charity hospitals and the municipality; joint appointments between the university and health service providers were a feature of the 1950s, and many people regretted their reduction. More generally, in the 1960s and 1970s, universities neglected their regional roles, but to some extent, since the 1990s, they have tended to re-focus on their immediate environments, even though the national Research Assessment Exercises, and increased competition between universities, have been pushing them in the opposite direction.

We have seen that relationships between the University and the public health organisations have usually been *ad hoc* and dependent on personal contacts and personalities; but some arrangements encourage such links, whilst others discourage them. Most NHS and local authorities now tend to buy research from consultants rather than universities, and this may be one reason why many reports on health and local economic development are so very repetitive, and why there is so little cumulation of information. British 'civic universities', of which Manchester was the premier example, developed as 'centres of intelligence' for their regions, and there would seem a real need for a reinstatement of that role, partly to secure stable centres of information, and deliberation, which are relatively independent of government fashions and peremptory demands.

Since the 1980s, local NHS public health staff have been relatively keen to collaborate with universities, though sometimes the time-horizons were difficult to match. But in this same period, university staff have been increasingly pressured to produce more and more publications – which does not help their work as teachers, still less their work on liaison and the improvement of local services. In all academic fields, publications tend to take precedence over wider scholarship and service work. This may not matter greatly in the natural sciences, but in social sciences and humanities, including some related to medicine, it tends to value small novelties rather than wider contributions, and topics that are fashionable among academics rather than ones which may be more useful. Universities and funding councils might well re-emphasise social utility, including regional roles, and not just intellectual fertility or media success.

British policy for higher education tends to contrast global aspirations and (merely) regional working. But this is in part a logical mistake. As the record of the Universities of California and Wisconsin well show, regional research can be every bit as demanding as other scales, and can be exceedingly useful well beyond the place of origin. Long term local 'conversations' between researchers and service providers are one path to wisdom; they were indeed one of the strengths of civic universities.

A more recent answer to the academic–service question has been the formation of networks, within and between universities, the NHS, and the city. Because the Manchester conurbation now has three universities, a range of new possibilities are added, which bring their own complications; likewise the growth of academic training and research in nursing and dentistry, and in several paramedical fields. How these many disciplines and local resources can be collectively mobilised in support of public health raises a difficult set of questions, for which incremental answers should draw carefully on past experience.

We have seen that regional networks for public health seem to have fared less well than initiatives focussed on a single city-region, notably Liverpool. Recent initiatives to bring together academic and NHS organisations across Manchester and Salford may help, though public health questions tend to be marginal to medical research and practice collaborations, for all the protestations to the contrary. One answer may be the North West Public Health Teaching Network, based at Manchester PCT, and currently funded as part of a new national programme to build public health capacity and capability.

But there is also much to be said for commitment from a major research university which can itself pull together a wide range of disciplines and regional information. Good staff from other universities or authorities in the region (or beyond) can be seconded or attached. There is no reason to privilege staff from the home institution; but there is reason to build a single core, over decades, closely allied to professional education of various kinds.

Here we may note that the University of Manchester presently boasts national leaders in several areas related to public health, including general practice, mental health services, occupational medicine, community nursing, infectious diseases, health service management, health inequalities (including ethnic dimensions), health politics, and medical informatics – but with relatively few interconnections, and without much focus on the city of Manchester as a subject of research and reform. Perhaps there is room for developing a school of public health on the scale characteristic of major American universities. It could be the point of reference for the social aspects of health, across all the relevant academic fields and professions – from dental hygiene to informatics, and from community nursing to epidemiology. Perhaps, as in other fields, the surest path is to connect and appoint top-quality researchers and organisers, linked with an observatory for the collection and analysis of health data, and with a unit for service-development in public health. It would succeed in as much as staff from other universities and agencies chose to spend their time there, as well as in their home institutions; and it would be asked to prove its worth by local studies, and 'action research', as well as by other publications.

Perhaps one fruit of this present historical work could be the establishment of a group to research such possibilities, and to share experience and knowledge, including best practices elsewhere. Such prospective research might itself build bridges and raise aspirations. By focussing intellectual and politic energy on public health in Manchester, it would be a suitable extension of our History.

Biographical Notes on People Interviewed

This is list of people interviewed for this book. The brief biographies focus on activities relevant to Manchester and/or public health. Unless indicated, all interviews were conducted by Emma Jones between November 2006 and January 2008.

Evelyn Asante–Mensah OBE was Chief Executive of the Black Health Agency, 1994–2006, a Non-Executive Director of Manchester Health Authority, 1998–2000, and Chair of Central Manchester Primary Care Trust, 2000–2006. She was appointed Chair of Manchester Primary Care Trust in October 2006, and is currently on secondment as a Strategic Advisor for community cohesion and diversity in the Government Office North West.

Prof. Leo Baric came to England from Croatia in March 1963 and shortly afterwards joined the Christie Social Research Unit in Manchester. He joined Manchester University in September 1965 as Assistant Lecturer in the Department of Social and Preventive Medicine and retired as a Reader in October 1988. He then joined the University of Salford as Professorial Fellow in Health Promotion and Health Education, teaching full-time in the Department for Environmental Studies, 1988–1998. After retiring from Salford, he was appointed Honorary Research Professor in the Dental School, University of Manchester.

Carol Baxter came to England from Jamaica to train as a nurse, midwife and health visitor. Following an M.Sc. in Community Medicine at the University of Manchester, 1978–1980, she worked in health education/health promotion for the Manchester Area Health Authority (Teaching), 1980–1982. She was a co-founder of Manchester Action Committee on

Healthcare for Ethnic Minorities (MACHEM) in 1978, acting as Chair until 1997. She is, at present, Head of Equality and Diversity at NHS Employers.

Dr Sally Bradley qualified as a doctor in Manchester, undertook further training in public health medicine in the North West, 1989–1993, and finished her GP training in West Yorkshire in 1995. She was Director of Public Health for Salford and Trafford Health Authority, 2000–2001 and Director of Public Health for Salford Primary Care Trust, 2002–2003. She was a principal in general practice in Salford and a GP with a special interest in public health at Salford Primary Care Trust. She was appointed Director of Public Health for Manchester Primary Care Trust in April 2007.

Dr Roger Brittain qualified as a doctor and gained his Masters in Public Health from the Department of Epidemiology and Public Health, Yale University Medical School in 1974. He was District Community Physician for North District, Manchester Area Health Authority (Teaching), 1979–1982. He held public health service and academic posts abroad, 1980–1982, and in North Warwickshire and Rugby Health Authorities, 1982–1992.

Michael Brown undertook the NHS graduate management entry scheme in London and was awarded his M.Sc. in Management Studies at Brunel University/Henley Management College in 1982. He held administrative and management posts in Durham, Birmingham and at University College Hospital, London, before becoming Administrator, and then Chief Executive, of North Manchester Health Authority, and later Chief Executive of South Manchester University Hospitals NHS Trust.

Theresa Chamberlain trained as a nurse at Withington Hospital, 1947–1952, first working at the Casualty Department of Ancoats Hospital in Manchester. She later trained as a district nurse and worked across Manchester and Oldham. After her retirement in 1987, she continued to work part-time, first as a Marie Curie nurse, and then for her local GP, for nine years.

Merryn Cooke trained as a nurse and health visitor in Manchester in the 1980s. She worked as a health visitor in Newton Heath in North Manchester for fourteen years from 1989. She then spent one year working in Brunswick. For the last three years she has worked part-time in Moss Side.

Prof. Kennedy Cruickshank qualified in medicine at the University of Birmingham, completing an epidemiological M.D. comparing diabetes and vascular disease in Caribbean-origin people between Jamaica and Britain. An M.Sc. in Epidemiology at the London School of Hygiene and Tropical Medicine was followed by a Wellcome Clinical Epidemiology Fellowship. He joined Manchester University Medical School as a Senior Lecturer in Clinical Epidemiology with Consultant Physician sessions in diabetes and hypertension. He is currently Professor of Cardiovascular Medicine and Clinical Epidemiology at the University of Manchester.

Prof. Stuart Donnan qualified as a doctor in Sydney, Australia and obtained his M.Sc. in Community Medicine from the London School of Hygiene and Tropical Medicine in 1973. After posts in Southampton, and at the Office of Population Census in London he was appointed to the Foundation Chair in the Department of Community Medicine in the Medical Faculty of the Chinese University of Hong Kong in 1981. He was Professor of Epidemiology and Public Health and Head of the Department of Community Medicine, later School of Epidemiology and Health Sciences, University of Manchester, 1990–1997.

Michael Eastwood qualified as a public health inspector in Liverpool in 1969 and was awarded the M.Sc. in Environmental Sciences from the University of Salford in 1973. After promotion within the Liverpool Public Health Department and academic posts in Perth, Western Australia, and Salford, he re-entered the service as Senior Assistant Director of Environmental Health for Manchester City Council in 1983 and was appointed Director of Environmental Health in 1985. He took early retirement in 1993.

Dr Peter Elton qualified as a doctor in Manchester and completed his M.Sc. in Community Medicine at the University of Manchester in 1980. He was a Consultant in Public Health Medicine, 1983–1992, and Director of Community Services, 1986–1992, for North Manchester Health Authority. He was a Consultant for Tameside and Glossop Health Authority/West Pennine Health Authority, 1992–1994/1995 and Director of Public Health for Wigan and Bolton Health Authority, 1995–2002. He is currently Director of Public Health for Bury Primary Care Trust.

Judith Emanuel studied for the M.Sc. in Community Medicine at the University of Manchester, 1979–1981. She worked for Manchester City Council as a community education worker in North Manchester,

1983–1985, moving to North Manchester Health Authority, first as a health promotion officer, 1985–1988, and then as Director of Health Promotion, 1988–1993. After leaving the NHS, she held various university posts including Lecturer in Public Health and Health Promotion, 1996–1999, and Lecturer in Education for Primary Health Care, 1999–2003, at the University of Manchester. She currently conducts independent research and evaluation, organisational development and training in the broad field of public health.

*Dr Neil Goodwin CBE is a leadership consultant and academic. He was Chief Executive of Manchester Health Authority, 1994–2001, Chief Executive of Greater Manchester Strategic Health Authority (SHA), 2002–2006, and Chief Executive lead for merging three Strategic Health Authorities to create the new North West Strategic Health Authority in July 2006. He holds a Ph.D. from the Manchester Business School.

Prof. Richard Heller qualified in clinical medicine, epidemiology and public health at the University of London, and held academic posts in London before moving to the University of Newcastle, Australia, where he was part of the International Clinical Epidemiology Network. In 2000, he was appointed Professor of Public Health at the University of Manchester, where he established the Evidence for Population Health Unit. He retired in 2006.

Dr Stephen Horsley qualified as a doctor in London in 1976 and did his public health training through the Northern Consortium. Following posts in Oxford and Cumbria he was Regional Medical Officer/Regional Director of Public Health for the North West Regional Health Authority, 1986–1994. He was a Consultant in Public Health Medicine for Morecambe Bay Health Authority, 1994–2000, and Director of the Public Health and Health Professional Development Unit at Lancaster University, 1995–2000. Since 2006 he has been Director of Public Health for Northamptonshire Primary Care Trust.

Dr Ann Hoskins qualified as a doctor at Queens University, Belfast. She worked in public health in the Republic of Yemen until 1991, in the meantime completing her M.Sc. in Public Health at the Liverpool School of Tropical Medicine. She was Director of Public Health for Wirral Health Authority, 1995–1998, Director of Public Health for Manchester Health Authority, 1998–2002 and Director of Public Health for Cumbria and Lancashire Strategic Health Authority, 2002–2006. She is currently Deputy Director of Public Health/Medical Director for NHS Northwest.

Dr Anna Elizabeth Jones was Deputy Senior Medical Officer for Manchester City Health Department, 1962–1967, and then Deputy Medical Officer of Health for Manchester, 1967–1974. She was District Community Physician for Central District, Manchester Area Health Authority (Teaching), 1974–1982, and later District Medical Officer for Central Manchester (District) Health Authority, 1982–1984. She was also Medical Officer for Environmental Health for Manchester, 1974–1984. She retired in 1984.

Prof. Ian Leck qualified as a doctor at the University of Birmingham, where he stayed as a research fellow before becoming Senior Lecturer in Community Medicine within the Medical Unit, University College Hospital Medical School, London, in 1966. He was appointed to the University of Manchester as a Reader in Social and Preventive Medicine (later Community Medicine) in 1971, and retired as Professor of Community Medicine and Head of the Department of Community Medicine at the University of Manchester in 1991.

★★Dr Joyce Leeson qualified as a doctor in Manchester in 1954, and completed a Diploma in Public Health at the Department of Social and Preventive Medicine in Manchester, in 1958. She was a researcher and later a Senior Lecturer within the department, 1965–1978. She was District Community Physician for South District, Manchester Area Health Authority (Teaching), 1978–1982, and District Medical Officer/Director of Public Health for North Manchester Health Authority, 1982–1992. She retired in 1992.

Cecilia Maxwell Bradley trained as a nurse, midwife and health visitor in Bolton, 1945–1954, and practised there as a health visitor and school nurse, 1954–1961. She joined the Manchester Local Authority Health Department as a Group Advisor in 1961, was promoted to the post of Deputy Superintendent Health Visitor in 1963, and was then Superintendent Health Visitor, 1964–1974. She became the first Area Nurse (Child Health) for Manchester Area Health Authority (Teaching), 1974–1982. She retired in 1982.

Prof. Joseph Moore joined the University of Manchester Dental School as Professor of Oral Surgery in 1966. He was Dean of the Manchester Dental School, 1968–1973, and Dean of the Manchester Medical School, 1976–1979. He has held many honorary NHS appointments including a member of Manchester Area Health Authority (Teaching), 1974–1976, Chair of North Manchester (District) Health Authority, 1981–1991, Chair of the Manchester Joint

Consultative Committee, 1984–1987, Chair of Manchester Purchasing Consortium, 1990–1993 and Chair of Central Manchester Health Authority, 1991–1994.

Jane Morris did a B.Sc. in Psychology and an M.Sc. by research on maternal and infant health inequalities under the supervision of Prof. Alwyn Smith at the University of Manchester. She was a Research Officer in the (South) Manchester Health Authorities and Teaching Hospitals' Department of Epidemiology and Social Research, 1983–1986, before moving to Manchester City Council, first as a health campaign worker, and later as Health Promotion Officer. She is currently Valuing Older People Research and Planning Officer, based within the Manchester Joint Health Unit.

Dr Michael Painter qualified as a doctor in London in 1973 and studied for the M.Sc. in Community Medicine at the University of Manchester, 1978–1980. He was Consultant in Public Health Medicine (Consultant in Communicable Disease Control) for Manchester, and Port Medical Officer and Port Medical Inspector, Manchester Airport, 1985–2004. In 2004–2005, he was Regional Epidemiologist for the Health Protection Agency in Greater Manchester. He is presently a Consultant Epidemiologist for the Health Protection Agency Centre for Infections in London.

Rev. Dr Peter Povey qualified as a doctor in Manchester in 1961 and was awarded his Diploma in Public Health from the University of Liverpool in 1968. He held medical officer posts at Warrington County Borough Health Department, and the Manchester and Liverpool Hospital Boards before his appointment as first Area Medical Officer for the Manchester Area Health Authority (Teaching), 1974–1982. He was District Medical Officer/Director of Public Health for Central Manchester Health Authority, 1982–1990, Director of Public Health for Bolton Health Authority, 1990–1994 and Director of Public Health for Wigan and Bolton Health Authority 1994–1995.

David Regan received his B.Sc. in psychology at the University of Newcastle upon Tyne in 1982 and the M.Sc. in Community Medicine at the University of Manchester in 1987. After research and senior health promotion posts in the North West, 1982–1989, he was Service Manager (HIV/GUM) for South Manchester Health Authority, 1989–1994, and later Public Health Specialist for Manchester Health Authority, 1994–2000. He was appointed Manchester Healthy City Co-ordinator in 2000. Since 2002, he has been Director of Manchester Joint Health Unit.

Eleanor Roaf did the M.Sc. in Public Health at the University of Manchester in 1989 after a first degree in philosophy and psychology. After working in research for the North West Regional Health Authority, she entered the Greater Manchester regional training programme for public health in 1995. She was a Consultant in Public Health for Bury Health Authority, later Bury Primary Care Trust, 1999–2002, and Director of Public Health for North Manchester Primary Care Trust, 2002–2006. She is currently a Public Health Consultant for Manchester Primary Care Trust.

Prof. Alwyn Smith CBE qualified as a doctor at the University of Birmingham and holds a Diploma in Public Health from the London School of Hygiene and Tropical Medicine. After academic posts in Singapore (for the WHO), Dundee, Edinburgh and Glasgow he joined the University of Manchester as Professor of Social and Preventive Medicine (later Community Medicine) and Head of Department in 1968. He became Professor of Epidemiology and Social Oncology and Head of the Unit based at the Christie Hospital in Manchester, in 1978. He retired in 1990.

Dr. Stephen Watkins qualified as a doctor in 1974. He took the M.Sc. in Community Medicine at the University of Manchester, 1979–1981. He held public health training posts in Blackburn, Salford, South Manchester and Oldham, and was a Consultant in Public Health in Oldham, 1984–1990. He has been Director of Public Health for Stockport Health Authority, later Primary Care Trust, since 1990.

★ Interviewed by Emma Jones and Stephanie Snow.
★★ Interviewed by John Pickstone and Emma Jones.

Department Structures

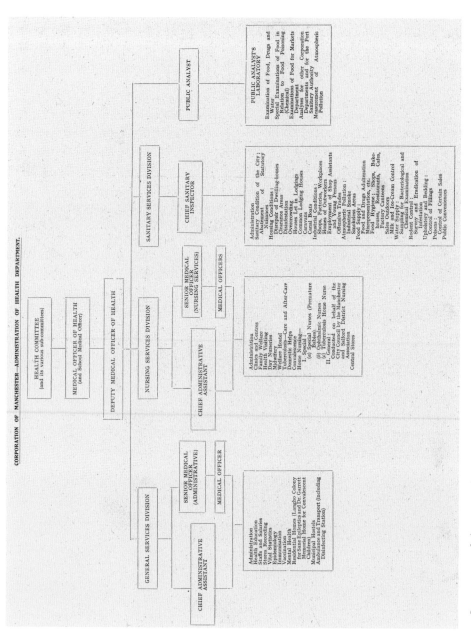

a. Structure of the Manchester Health Department, 1952. Source: Manchester MOH Report, 1952.

Medical Officer of Health

Deputy Medical Officer of Health

Departmental Management and Administration

- Management and budgetary control
- Committee information and instructions
- Forward planning and development of services
- Personnel, training and manpower planning
- Secretarial, administration and clerical services and procedures
- Statistics
- Management and organisational development and techniques
- Physical resources (premises, supplies etc.)
- Planned programming budgeting

Environmental and Protection Health Services		
Principal Medical Officer	**Chief Public Health Inspector**	
Epidemiology	Public health inspection	
Immunisation and disease prevention	Housing – pest control	
Health statistics	Food and drugs; Food hygiene	
Airport health control	Clean air – caravan sites	
Ambulance service	Occupational hygiene; Shops Act	
Staff health, hygiene and welfare	Public Conveniences	
Radioactivity	**Chief Veterinary Officer**	
Unfit housing inspection	Meat inspection service	
Re-housing for medical reasons	Veterinary services	
	Public Analyst	
	Food – Drugs samples	
	Port Health etc. – samples	

Personal Health Services		
Principal Medical Officer	**Principal Medical Officer**	
Health centres	School medical examinations	
Care of mothers and young children	Handicapped children	
Family welfare	Minor ailments clinic	
Family planning	Special clinics (ear, nose, throat and Ophthalmic)	
Pre-symptomatic diagnosis	Child guidance	
Dialysis	Speech therapy	
Chiropody	Physiotherapy	
Prevention of illness, care and aftercare	Convalescence	
Midwifery	Audiology	
Health Visiting	**Principal Dental Officer**	
Home nursing	School dental service	
	Dental care of mothers and young children	

b. Structure of the Manchester Health Department, 1972. Source: Manchester MOH Report, 1952.

© MANCHESTER CITY COUNCIL

NHS Re-organisations in Manchester, 1974–2006

1974 – Establishment of Manchester Area Health Authority (Teaching)

1982 – Abolition of Manchester Area Health Authority (Teaching) and creation of North, Central and South Manchester District Health Authorities

1991 – Reconfiguration of three District Health Authorities as Health Authorities; introduction of the Purchaser/Provider split

1994 – Merger of three Health Authorities to create Manchester Health Authority

1999 – Formation of North, South, East and West Manchester Primary Care Groups

2002 – Abolition of Manchester Health Authority and creation of North, Central and South Manchester Primary Care Trusts; Manchester Joint Health Unit established

2006 – Merger of Primary Care Trusts to form Manchester Primary Care Trust

Notes

CHAPTER TWO: FROM THE INDUSTRIAL REVOLUTION TO
THE WELFARE STATE

1. For general histories of nineteenth-century public health, see G. Rosen,
   History of Public Health (New York, 1958); C. F. Brockington, *Public
   Health in the Nineteenth Century* (Edinburgh, 1965); and A. S. Wohl,
   Endangered Lives: Public Health in Victorian Britain (London, 1983). For
   public health in nineteenth-century Manchester, see J. V. Pickstone,
   *Medicine and Industrial Society: A History of Hospital Development in
   Manchester and its Region, 1752–1946* (Manchester, 1985) and *Bulletin of the
   John Rylands University Library of Manchester*, 87:1 (2005). For the history
   of Manchester in general, see A. J. Kidd, *Manchester* (Edinburgh, 2002).

2. J. V. Pickstone, 'Dearth, Dirt and Fever Epidemics: Rewriting the
   History of British Public Health, 1780–1850', in T. Ranger and P. Slack
   (eds), *Epidemics and Ideas: Essays on the Historical Perception of Pestilence*
   (Cambridge, 1992), 125–148.

3. J. V. Pickstone, 'Ferriar's Fever to Kay's Cholera: Disease and Social
   Structure in Cottonopolis', *History of Science*, 22 (1984), 401–419.

4. J. V. Pickstone and S. V. F. Butler, 'The Politics of Medicine in the Early
   Industrial City: A Study of Hospital Reform and Medical Relief in Late
   Eighteenth-Century Manchester', *Medical History*, 28 (1984), 227–249.

5. J. V. Pickstone, 'Thomas Percival and the Production of Medical Ethics',
   in R. Baker, D. Porter and R. Porter (eds), *The Codification of Medical
   Morality* (Amsterdam, 1993), pp. 161–178.

6. Pickstone, 'Ferriar's Fever to Kay's Cholera'.

7. On Chadwick see S. E. Finer, *The Life and Times of Edwin Chadwick*
   (London & New York, 1952, 1970); R. A. Lewis, *Edwin Chadwick and
   the Public Health Movement, 1832–1854* (London, 1952); and especially
   C. Hamlin, *Public Health and Social Justice in the Age of Chadwick: Britain,
   1800–1854* (Cambridge, 1998).

8. E. C. Midwinter, *Social Administration in Lancashire, 1830–1860* (Manchester, 1969).

9. Hamlin, *Public Health and Social Justice in the Age of Chadwick.*

10. A. Wilson, 'Technology and Municipal Decision-Making: Sanitary Systems in Manchester, 1868–1910', University of Manchester Ph.D. Thesis (1990).

11. J. Mottram, 'The Life and Work of John Roberton MRCS LSA, (1797–1876)', University of Manchester Institute of Science and Technology M.Sc. Thesis (1973).

12. On the early history of the University see H. B. Charlton, *Portrait of a University, 1851–1951: to Commemorate the Centenary of Manchester University* (Manchester, 1952).

13. V. Heggie, 'Re-imagining the Healthy Social Body: Medicine, Welfare and Health Reform in Manchester, 1880–1910', University of Manchester Ph.D. Thesis (2004).

14. Wilson, 'Technology and Municipal Decision-Making'.

15. G. Searle, *The Search for National Efficiency* (Oxford, 1971).

16. Heggie, 'Re-imagining the Healthy Social Body'.

17. Wilson, 'Technology and Municipal Decision-Making'. On public health and sanitary expenditure, see F. Bell and R. Millward, 'Public Health Expenditures and Mortality in England and Wales, 1870–1914', *Continuity and Change*, 13:2 (1998), 221–249.

18. A. Redford, *The History of Local Government in Manchester*, 3 Volumes (London, 1939–1940); H. Ritvo, *The Dawn of Green: Manchester, Thirlmere, and the Victorian Environment* (Chicago, forthcoming).

19. C. Rowley, *Fifty Years of Work without Wages* (London, 1912).

20. J. C. Thresh, *An Inquiry into the Causes of Excessive Mortality in No. 1 District, Ancoats* (Manchester, 1889).

21. For a discussion of Rowley, Thresh and reform in Manchester see H. L. Platt, 'From Hygeia to the Garden City: Bodies, Houses, and the Re-discovery of the Slum in Manchester, 1875–1910', *Journal of Urban History*, 35:5 (2002), 756–772.

22. Rowley, *Fifty Years of Work without Wages*, pp. 151–160.

23. E. Gauldie, *Cruel Habitations: A History of Working-Class Housing, 1780–1918* (New York, 1974).

24. M. Worboys, *Spreading Germs: Disease Theories and Medical Practice in Britain, 1865–1900* (Cambridge, 2000).

25. J. Niven, *Observations on the History of Public Health Effort in Manchester* (Manchester, 1923).

26. See article on S. Delépine in J. Willis-Ellwood and F. Tuxford (eds), *Some Manchester Doctors: A Biographical Collection to mark the 150th Anniversary of the Manchester Medical Society, 1834–1984* (Manchester, 1984).

27. M. Jackson, *The Borderland of Imbecility: Medicine, Society and the Fabrication of the Feeble Mind in Late Victorian and Edwardian England* (Manchester, 2000).

28. J. Barclay, 'Langho Epileptic Colony, 1906–1984: A Contextual Study of the Origins, Transformations and Demise of Manchester's Colony for Sane Pauper Epileptics', University of Manchester Ph.D. Thesis (1988).

29. Pickstone, *Medicine and Industrial Society*, ch. 10.

30. J. Mottram, 'State Control in Local Context: Public Health and Midwifery Regulation in Manchester, 1900–1914', in H. Marland and A. M. Rafferty (eds), *Midwives, Society and Childbirth: Debates and Controversies in the Modern Period* (London, 1997).

31. S. Simon, *A Century of City Government, Manchester, 1838–1938* (London, 1938).

32. E. D. Simon, *A City Council from Within* (London, 1926); Simon, *A Century of City Government*.

CHAPTER THREE: POST–WAR PUBLIC HEALTH: FROM THE INTRODUCTION OF THE NHS TO ITS RE–ORGANISATION IN 1974

1. R. Bud, *Penicillin: Triumph and Tragedy* (Oxford, 2007).

2. On the development of the NHS see C. Webster, *The Health Services since the War. Vol. 1. Problems of Health Care: The National Health Service before 1957* (London, 1988).

3. M. J. Daunton, 'Payment and Participation: Welfare and State-Formation in Britain, 1900–1951', *Past and Present*, 150 (February 1996), 169–216.

4. R. D. Putnam, *Bowling Alone: The Collapse and Revival of American Community* (New York, 2000).

5. J. V. Pickstone, 'Medicine in Manchester: Manchester in Medicine, 1750–2005', *Bulletin of the John Rylands University Library of Manchester*, 87:1 (2005), pp. 28–34.

6. J. Anderson, F. Neary and J. V. Pickstone, *Surgeons, Manufacturers and Patients: A Transatlantic History of Total Hip Replacement* (Basingstoke, 2007).

7. J. V. Pickstone, 'Psychiatry in District General Hospitals: History, Contingency and Local Innovation in the Early Years of the National Health Service', in J. V. Pickstone (ed.), *Medical Innovations in Historical Perspective* (Basingstoke, 1992).

8. J. Lewis, *What Price Community Medicine? The Philosophy, Practice, and Politics of Public Health since 1919* (Brighton, 1986); C. Webster, *The Health Services since the War. Vol. 2. Government and Health Care: The National Health Service, 1958–1979* (London, 1996).

9. J. Welshman, 'The Medical Officer of Health in England and Wales, 1900–1974: Watchdog or Lapdog?', *Journal of Public Health Medicine*, 19:4 (1997), 443–450; L. Diack and D. F. Smith, 'Professional Strategies of Medical Officers of Health in the Post-War Period – 1: 'Innovative Traditionalism': The Case of Dr Ian MacQueen, MOH for Aberdeen 1952–1974, a 'Bull-Dog' with the 'Hide of a Rhinoceros'', *Journal of Public Health Medicine*, 24:2 (2002), 123–129; S. McLaurin and D. F. Smith, 'Professional Strategies of Medical Officers of Health in the Post-War Period – 2: 'Progressive Realism': The Case of Dr R. J. Donaldson, MOH for Teesside, 1968–1974', *Journal of Public Health Medicine*, 24:2 (2002), 130–135.

10. Manchester Medical Officer of Health (MOH) Report, 1947.

11. C. Metcalfe Brown, 'The Officer of Health', *Public Health*, 60 (December 1946), p. 51.

12. Manchester MOH Report, 1948.

13. C. Metcalfe Brown, 'The National Public Health Service', *Public Health*, 67 (October 1953), p. 2.

14. H. Freeman, 'Mental Health Services in an English County Borough (Salford)', *Medical History*, 28 (1984), 111–128.

15. Pickstone, 'Psychiatry in District General Hospitals'.

16. Manchester MOH Report, 1958; re-quoted from Manchester MOH Report, 1942.

17. Manchester MOH Reports, 1957 and 1962.

18. 'Letters to the Editor', *The Lancet* (15 October 1955), p. 821.

19. Manchester MOH Report, 1954, p. 161.

20. S. Mosley, *The Chimney of the World: A History of Smoke Pollution in Victorian and Edwardian Manchester* (Cambridge, 2001), p. 186. In 1976, the Council celebrated Manchester's efforts in the implementation of clean air since the 1950s in Manchester Area Council for Clean Air and Noise Control, *Twenty Years Review of Air Pollution in the Area of the Council* (Manchester, 1976).

21. Manchester Environmental Health Department Annual Report, 1976, p. 6.

22. Manchester MOH Reports, 1956 and 1962.

23. Manchester MOH Report, 1957, p. 141.

24. N. E. Lingard, *Family Welfare Centre: An Account of the Work Done in the Manchester Family Welfare Centre from its Beginnings in 1948 to the Present Time When it has Become a Recognised Branch of the Public Health Service* (Manchester, 1960).

25. Manchester MOH Report, 1957, p. 110.

26. Manchester MOH Report, 1957, p. 111; Manchester MOH Report, 1966, p. 92.

27. Manchester MOH Report, 1965, p. 97.

28. Manchester MOH Report, 1962, p. 96.

29. Manchester MOH Report, 1963, p.86; Manchester MOH Report, 1964, p. 92.

30. Manchester MOH Report, 1966, p. 7.

31. Manchester MOH Report, 1949.

32. Metcalfe Brown, 'The Officer of Health', p. 53.

33. Manchester MOH Report, 1966, pp. 13–14.

34. For more information on the MCC's educational experiment see E. Toon, '"Cancer as the General Population Knows It": Knowledge, Fear, and Lay Education in 1950s Britain', *Bulletin of the History of Medicine*, 81:1 (2007), 116–138. See also, J. Wakefield, *Cancer and Public Education* (London, 1962).

35. J. Wakefield (ed.), *Seek Wisely to Prevent: Studies of Attitudes and Action in a Cervical Cytology Programme* (London, 1972).

36. A. E. Jones and C. Metcalfe Brown, 'Screening for Cancer of the Cervix at Local Authority Clinics in Manchester', *The Lancet* (6 March, 1965), 543.

37. The programme was broadcast on 25 January 1966; Manchester MOH Report, 1967.

38. For a brief history of the development of the public health school and laboratory at Manchester see E. H. Walker, 'The Manchester School of Public Health, Abridgement of Presidential Address to the North-Western Branch of Medical Officers of Health', *Public Health*, 61 (December 1947), 39–40.

39. The University of Manchester, The John Rylands University Library, Vice-Chancellor's Archive (VCA)/7/74, notes on Preventive Medicine, 15 February 1946.

40. A. Topping, 'Maternal Mortality and Public Opinion', *Public Health*, 49 (July 1936), 342–349.

41. A. Topping, 'Prevention – Medical and Economic. Presidential Address to the Society of Medical Officers of Health, London, 17 September 1952', *Public Health* (November 1952), p. 17.

42. VCA/7/578, letter from A. Topping to J. Stopford, 30 December 1949.

43. C. Hallet, 'Colin Fraser Brockington (1903–2004) and the Revolution in Nurse-Education', *Journal of Medical Biography*, 16 (2008), 89–95.

44. Interview with Emeritus Prof. I. Leck.

45. VCA/7/187, memoranda and curriculum outline.

46. See, for example, E. T. Chester and J. H. Smith, *Management Under Nationalisation. Studies in Decentralisation* (London: Acton Society Trust, 1953).

47. C. F. Brockington, 'The Need for a Revision in the Training of Health Visitors', *Public Health* (April 1949), 144–146.

48. C. Hallett, 'The 'Manchester Scheme': A Study of the Diploma in Community Nursing, the first Pre-Registration Nursing Programme in a British University', *Nursing Inquiry*, 12:4 (2005), p. 289.

49. VCA/7/187, course for nurse tutors held 1–4 November 1953.

50. Hallett, 'The 'Manchester Scheme', p. 292.

51. Lewis, *What Price Community Medicine*, pp. 57–59.

52. Webster, *The Health Services since the War. Vol. 1*, pp. 380–388.

53. Manchester MOH Report, 1965.

54. C. F. Brockington, 'The Teaching of the Medical Student in Community Health. Presidential Address to the Teaching Group of the Society of Medical Officers of Health, Manchester, 14 April 1957', *Public Health*, 71:8 (1957), 301–306.

55. M. Perry, 'A Teaching Health Centre in Manchester: Medical Education and General Practice, 1943–1954', University of Manchester MA (Econ.) Dissertation (1996), pp. 37–57.

56. C. F. Brockington, 'Partners in Social Medicine', *Public Health*, 74:2 (1959), 69–71.

57. See M. Perry, 'Academic General Practice in Manchester under the Early National Health Service: A Failed Experiment in Social Medicine', *Journal of Social History of Medicine*, 13:1 (2000), 111–129.

58. VCA/7/187, newspaper clipping.

59. Office of the President and Vice-Chancellor, University of Manchester, (VCA)/3/39, letter from G. E. Godber to the Vice-Chancellor, 31 December 1963.

60. VCA/3/39, letter from Mervyn Susser to the Vice-Chancellor, June 1966; Susser believes his appointment was opposed by the professor of Psychiatry, who also had South African connections; interview with Mervyn Susser, conducted by John Pickstone.

61. C. Cook, 'Oral History – Professor Alwyn Smith', *Journal of Public Health*, 27 (2005), p.136; VCA/3/39, curriculum vitae of Alwyn Smith.

62. Interview with Prof. A. Smith.

63. Hallet, 'The Manchester Scheme', p. 292.

64. 'Report of BMA Working Party on the Medical Examination of Immigrants', *British Medical Journal*, 2:5475 (11 December 1965), 1423–1424.

65. Manchester MOH Report, 1970.

66. Manchester MOH Report, 1970.

67. A. Leathard, *The Fight for Family Planning: The Development of Family Planning Services in Britain, 1921–74* (London, 1980), p. 162.

68. Manchester MOH Report, 1972.

69. P. Shapley, D. Tanner, and A. Walling, 'Civic Culture and Housing Policy in Manchester, 1945–1979', *Twentieth-Century British History*, 15:4 (2004), pp. 424–429.

CHAPTER FOUR: A RE-ORGANISED NHS, 1974–1990

1. The post of District Community Physician (DCP) for North Manchester

was vacant until 1979, when Dr Roger Brittain was appointed. Dr D. J. Roberts was DCP for South Manchester from 1974 to 1976. From 1976 until 1978 the post lay vacant until Dr Joyce Leeson was appointed.

2. Interviews with Dr A. E. Jones and C. Maxwell Bradley. The Local Authority had originally endorsed the Joint Liaison Committee's recommendation that Manchester be divided into four districts: North, South, Central and Wythenshawe. Another idea had been to have two districts, and one central administrative level of the Area; see Manchester Health Committee Minutes, Volume 74, appendix 20, 1973.

3. Figures taken from Lewis, *What Price Community Medicine*, pp. 138 and 153.

4. V. Berridge, D. A. Christie and E. M. Tansey, *Public health in the 1980s and 1990s: Decline and Rise? Wellcome Witnesses to Twentieth Century Medicine*, Vol. 26 (Wellcome Trust Centre for the History of Medicine at UCL, 2006), p. 21.

5. V. Berridge, *Health and Society in Britain since 1939* (Cambridge, 1999), pp. 87–89.

6. The records of the Politics of Health Group are held at the Wellcome Library in London.

7. L. Baric, 'Health Education and the Smoking Habit', *Health Education Journal*, 37:1 (1978), 132–137.

8. V. Berridge, *Marketing Health: Smoking and the Discourse of Public Health in Britain, 1945–2000* (Oxford, 2007).

9. The BMA wrote Baric a letter stating as such; interview with Prof. L. Baric.

10. Detailed, personal accounts of the work of North Manchester Health Authority, written by Prof. J. Moore and M. Brown, will be included in the archive of interview material for this project.

11. Interview with Dr J. Leeson.

12. See V. Harrington, 'Voices Beyond the Asylum: A Post-War History of Mental Health Services in Manchester and Salford', University of Manchester Ph.D. Thesis (2008).

13. On the establishment of Well Women Clinics in the Wythenshawe, Withington and Rusholme districts of Manchester see J. Orr (ed.), *Women's Health in the Community* (Chichester, 1987), chs 7, 8 and 9.

14. S. Cawley, A. Martin, A. Inman and P. Muttram, 'North Manchester: Women's Health at Risk', in D. Seedhouse and A. Cribb, *Changing Ideas in Health Care* (Chichester, 1989), pp. 159–176.

15. E. Sherlock, 'The Liverpool Experience: The Croxteth Women's Health Group: Self-Help in a Deprived Community of Liverpool', in Orr, *Women's Health*, pp. 153–166.

16. Interview with J. Emanuel.

17. Interview with Prof. J. Moore and M. Brown.

18. 'From Crisis in Caring to the Best of Health: National Health Service', *Sunday Times*, 11 September 1988.

19. Manchester Environmental Health Department Annual Report, 1975, pp. 4–11.

20. The Annual Report for 1985 recorded a workforce of 473 persons, ranging from directors to manual and part-time staff.

21. Manchester Environmental Health Department Annual Report, 1984/1985.

22. Manchester Environmental Health Department Annual Report, 1976.

23. Manchester Environmental Health Department Annual Report, 1980.

24. P. Shapley, 'Tenants Arise! Consumerism, Tenants and the challenge of Council Authority in Manchester, 1968–92', *Social History*, 31:1 (2006), 60–78.

25. Manchester Environmental Health Department Annual Report, 1979.

26. B. Robson, 'Mancunian Ways: The Politics of Regeneration', in J. Peck and K. Ward (eds), *City of Revolution: Restructuring Manchester* (Manchester, 2002), p. 35; also see, in the same volume, S. Quilley, 'Entrepreneurial Turns: Municipal Socialism and After', pp. 76–94.

27. Manchester Environmental Health Department Annual Report, 1984/5.

28. V. Berridge (ed.), 'Witness Seminar: The Black Report and the Health Divide', in V. Berridge and S. Blume (eds), *Poor Health: Social Inequality before and after the Black Report* (London, 2003), pp. 131–171.

29. Berridge and Blume, *Poor Health*.

30. Manchester Joint Consultative Committee (Health) / City Planning Department, *Health Inequalities and Manchester* (Manchester, 1986), pp. 1–2.

31. North Manchester Health Authority, Public Health Report, December 1990, p. 51.

32. V. Berridge, *Aids in the UK: The Making of Policy 1981–1994* (Oxford, 1996).

33. 'Health Chief's New AIDS Row', *Manchester Evening News*, 18 November 1985, p. 9.

34. 'AIDS Law Not to be Used', *Daily Telegraph*, 19 October 1986, p. 8.

35. 'Health Chief's New AIDS Row', *Manchester Evening News*, 18 November 1985, p. 9.

36. 'City Defends AIDS Charter', *Manchester Evening News*, 6 November 1986, p. 4.

37. North Manchester Health Authority, Public Health Report, December 1990, p. 51.

38. J. Ashton, and H. Seymour, *The New Public Health: The Liverpool Experience* (Milton Keynes, 1988), pp. 136–151.

39. In 1985, the Terrence Higgins Trust decided not to set up a North West branch; the nearest branch to Manchester is in Leeds. A History of

George House Trust can be found on the Trust's website at http://www. ght.org.uk/ght/inside_ght_history.php.

40. J. Leeson, 'Health for All – Lessons from HIV/AIDS. Reflections of a Jobbing Public Health Doctor', *Public Health*, 105:1 (1991), p. 52; emphasis in original.

41. H. Valier and R. Bivins, 'Organisation, Ethnicity and the British National Health Service', in J. Stanton (ed.), *Innovations in Health and Medicine* (London, 2002), pp. 37–64.

42. A detailed account by one of the original founders of MACHEM can be found in G. Ferguson, 'The MACHEM Experience', in S. Rawaf and V. Bahl (eds), *Assessing Health Needs of People from Minority Ethnic Groups* (London, 1998), pp. 307–318.

43. This came about as a result of the sudden death of the Director of the Social Research Unit, Dr John Wakefield, in January 1978, which led to a review of the work of the unit and its amalgamation with the Regional Cancer Epidemiology Unit. The Chair was funded by NHS sources.

44. VCA/3/142, confidential memorandum sent to the Registrar from the Departmental Board of Department of Community Medicine, no date.

45. VCA/3/142, confidential memorandum sent to the Registrar from the Departmental Board of Department of Community Medicine, no date.

46. VCA/3/142, letter from A. J. Lane to Prof. J. R. Moore, 5 July 1978.

47. The change also brought unforeseen consequences for staff as academic salaries in public health lagged behind those in the NHS, despite the clinical status.

48. B. Pullan and M. Abendstern, *A History of the University of Manchester, 1973–1990* (Manchester, 2004), p. 251.

CHAPTER FIVE: THE 1990S: PUBLIC HEALTH AND NEO-LIBERALISM

1. Central Manchester Health Authority, Report of the Director of Public Health, 1990.

2. Leeson, 'Health For All', p. 54.

3. V. Berridge, 'Multidisciplinary Public Health: What Sort of Victory', *Public Health*, 121:6 (2007), 404–408.

4. Central Manchester Health Authority, Annual Report, 1991/1992.

5. Central Manchester Health Authority, Annual Report, 1992/1993.

6. Central Manchester Health Authority, Report of the Director of Public Health, 1992, p. 11.

7. These were North 1: Blackley, Central, Cheetham, Crumpsall; North 2: Beswick and Clayton, Bradford, Charlestown, Harpurhey, Lightbowne,

Moston, Newton Heath; Central 1: Ardwick, Fallowfield, Hulme, Moss Side, Rusholme; Central 2: Burnage, Gorton North, Gorton South, Levenshulme, Longsight; South 1: Barlow Moor, Chorlton, Didsbury, Old Moat, Whalley Range, Withington; South 2: Baguley, Benchill, Brooklands, Northenden, Sharston, Woodhouse Park.

8. On this, see M. Fotaki, 'Can Directors of Public Health Implement the New Public Health Agenda in Primary Care? A Case Study of Primary Care Trusts in the North West of England', *Policy and Politics*, 35:2 (2007), 311–335.

9. Quilley, 'Entrepreneurial Turns', p. 85.

10. R. Johnson, 'Manchester Health Authority, 1995 to 2002 – A Balanced Scorecard?' (Manchester NHS, 2002).

11. Manchester Health Authority, Annual Public Health Report, 1997/1998.

12. M. Barnes, H. Sullivan and E. Matka, 'The Development of Collaborative Capacity in Health Action Zones: A Final Report from the National Evaluation' (University of Birmingham, 2004).

13. List of members courtesy of M. Eastwood.

14. Pullan and Abendstern, *History of the University*, p. 248.

15. The University of Manchester, The John Rylands University Library, Archives of the Manchester Medical Society: Section of Community Medicine (MMS)/2/9/1/1, council minutes, 21 January 1986.

16. MMS/2/9/1/1, council minutes, 13 January 1997, 12 January 1998 and 11 May 1998.

CHAPTER SIX: PUBLIC HEALTH IN THE TWENTY FIRST CENTURY

1. Manchester City Council and Manchester NHS Primary Care Trust, Manchester Public Health Annual Report, 2006, p. 4.

2. Fotaki, 'Can Directors of Public Health Implement the New Public Health Agenda', p. 318.

3. Audit Commission, 'Greater Manchester Health Inequalities Review: Greater Manchester Health Leadership Network', Audit 2005/2006 and 2006/2007, p. 10.

4. D. J. Hunter and S. O'Toole, 'Manchester Joint Health Unit' (University of Durham, Business School, December 2000).

5. Further information about the Joint Health Unit can be found on its website: http://www.manchester.gov.uk/health/jhu/

6. Interview with Dr J. Leeson.

7. Interview with Dr S. Watkins.

1. See Pickstone and Butler, 'The Politics of Medicine in the Early Industrial City'; Pickstone 'Thomas Percival'. In general, the references for this concluding chapter can be found in the main text, and have only been repeated here for key arguments.

2. Pickstone, 'Dearth, Dirt and Fever Epidemics'.

3. For the likely effect of lifestyle improvement on medical costs see A. S. St Leger, 'Would a Healthier Population Consume Fewer Health Service Resources? A Life-Table Analysis using Hospital In-Patient Enquiry (HIPE) Bed-Usage Statistics as a Proxy for Hospital Treatment Costs' *International Journal of Epidemiology*, 18 (1989), 227–31. The cost of medical care over the life-time of an individual is now heavily concentrated in the last year of life.

4. For an introduction to some of the literature on Manchester and economic development see, Peck and Ward, *City of Revolution*. For a major study on 2008–2009, see The Manchester Independent Economic Review sponsored by Manchester Enterprises; see http://www.manchester-review.org.uk.

5. Derek Wanless, *Securing Good Health for the Whole Population*, (2004), p. 52.

6. See S. R. Harrison and R. Macdonald, *The Politics of Healthcare in Britain* (London, 2008), p. 11.

7. For the history of the Manchester medical elite and their roles around the Second World War, see H. K. Valier and J. V. Pickstone, *Community, Professions and Business: a History of the Central Manchester Teaching Hospitals and the National Health Service*, published by Central Manchester and Manchester Children's University Hospital NHS Trust, in association with the Centre for the History of Science, Technology and Medicine, University of Manchester, 2008.

8. For the rather different forms of politics in Scotland and Wales see S. Greer, *Divergence and Devolution* (London, 2001).

9. Wanless, p. 110.

10. Wanless, p. 162.

11. R. S. Bhopal and J. Last (eds), *Public health: Past, Present and Future: Celebrating Academic Public Health in Edinburgh, 1902–2002* (London 2004).

Bibliography

Sources consulted

Manchester Local Studies Library and Archives
Environmental Health Department Annual Reports, 1974–1985
Health Authority Annual Reports and Public Health Annual Reports,
    Manchester, (various), 1974–2002
Manchester Medical Officer of Health Reports, 1869–1973
Records of the Manchester Cleansing Department: Committee Minutes,
    1945–1973

Manchester PCT Library
Manchester NHS Primary Care Trust Annual Reports, 2002–2006

*The University of Manchester: The John Rylands University Library,
Special Collections / The Office of the President and Vice-Principal*
Vice-Chancellor's Archive
Archives of the Manchester Medical Society

Selected Reading

Books and Published Reports

Ashton J., and Seymour, H. *The New Public Health: The Liverpool Experience*
    (Milton Keynes: Open University Press, 1988).
Berridge, V., and Blume, S. (eds) *Poor Health: Social Inequality before and after
    the Black Report* (London: Frank Cass, 2003).
——, Christie, D. A., and Tansey, E. M. (eds) *Public health in the 1980s and
    1990s: Decline and Rise? Wellcome Witnesses to Twentieth Century Medicine*,
    Vol. 26 (Welcome Trust Centre for the History of Medicine at UCL,
    2006).
Brockington, C. F. *Public Health in the Nineteenth Century* (Edinburgh &
    London: E. & S. Livingstone Ltd., 1965).

Charlton, H. B. *Portrait of a University, 1851–1951: to Commemorate the Centenary of Manchester University* (Manchester: Manchester University Press, 1952).

Harrison, S. R., and Macdonald, R. *The Politics of Healthcare in Britain* (London: Sage Publications, 2008).

Kidd, A. J. *Manchester* (Keele: Keele University Press, 1993).

Lingard, N. E. *Family Welfare Centre: An Account of the Work Done in the Manchester Family Welfare Centre from its Beginnings in 1948 to the Present Time When it has Become a Recognised Branch of the Public Health Service* (Manchester: Manchester Family Welfare Centre, 1960).

Manchester Area Council for Clean Air and Noise Control, *Twenty Years Review of Air Pollution in the Area of the Council* (Manchester: Manchester Town Hall, 1976).

Manchester Joint Consultative Committee (Health), *Health Inequalities and Manchester* (Manchester: Manchester City Council, 1986).

Mosley, S. *The Chimney of the World: A History of Smoke Pollution in Victorian and Edwardian Manchester* (Cambridge: White Horse, 2001).

Niven, J. *Observations on the History of Public Health Effort in Manchester* (Manchester: John Heywood Ltd., 1923).

Peck, J., and Ward, K. (eds) *City of Revolution: Restructuring Manchester* (Manchester: Manchester University Press, 2002).

Pickstone, J. V. *Medicine and Industrial Society: A History of Hospital Development in Manchester and its Region, 1752–1946* (Manchester: Manchester University Press, 1985).

Pickstone, J. V., and Butler, S. V. F. (eds) *Medical History in Manchester: Health and Healing in an Industrial City, 1750–2005* (Manchester: The John Rylands University Library, 2007)

Pullan, P., and Abendstern, M. A. *History of the University of Manchester, 1973–1990* (Manchester: Manchester University Press, 2004).

Rowley, C. *Fifty Years of Work without Wages* (London: Hodder and Stoughton, 1912).

Stevens, R. (ed.) *Health Inequalities and Manchester in the 1990s* (Manchester: Manchester Health For All Working Party, 1993).

Thresh, J. C. *An Inquiry into the Causes of Excessive Mortality in No. 1 District, Ancoats* (Manchester: Heywood, 1889).

Valier, H. K., and Pickstone, J. V. *Community, Professions and Business: A History of the Central Manchester Teaching Hospitals and the National Health Service* (Manchester: Central Manchester and Manchester Children's University Hospital NHS Trust, in association with the Centre for the History of Science, Technology and Medicine, University of Manchester, 2008. Distributed by Carnegie Publishing, 01524 840111. www.carnegiepublishing.com)

Wanless, D. *Securing Our Future Health: Taking a Long-Term View* (HM Treasury, 2002).

——, *Securing Good Health for the Whole Population* (HM Treasury, 2004).

Webster, C. *The Health Services since the War. Vol. 1. Problems of Health Care: The National Health Service before 1957* (London: HMSO, 1988).

——, *The Health Services since the War. Vol. 2. Government and Health Care the National Health Service, 1958–1979* (London: HMSO, 1996).

Willis-Ellwood, J., and Tuxford, F. (eds) *Some Manchester Doctors: A Biographical Collection to mark the 150th Anniversary of the Manchester Medical Society, 1834–1984* (Manchester: Manchester University Press, 1984).

Articles

Baric, L. 'Health Education and the Smoking Habit', *Health Education Journal*, 37:1 (1978), 132–137.

Brockington, C. F. 'The Need for a Revision in the Training of Health Visitors', *Public Health* (April 1949), 144–146.

——, 'The Teaching of the Medical Student in Community Health. Presidential Address to the Teaching Group of the Society of Medical Officers of Health, Manchester, 14 April 1957', *Public Health*, 71:8 (1957), 301–306.

——, 'Partners in Social Medicine', *Public Health*, 74:2 (1959), 69–71.

Cawley, S., Martin, A., Inman, A., and Muttram, P. 'North Manchester: Women's Health at Risk', in D. Seedhouse and A. Cribb (eds), *Changing Ideas in Health Care* (Chichester: Wiley, 1989), pp.159–176.

Cook, C. 'Oral History – Professor Alwyn Smith', *Journal of Public Health*, 27 (2005), 135–142.

Ferguson, G. 'The MACHEM Experience', in S. Rawaf and V. Bahl (eds), *Assessing Health Needs of People from Minority Ethnic Groups* (London: Royal College of Physicians, 1998), pp.307–318.

Hallett, C. 'The 'Manchester Scheme': A Study of the Diploma in Community Nursing, the First Pre-Registration Nursing Programme in a British University', *Nursing Inquiry*, 12:4 (2005), 287–294.

——, 'Colin Fraser Brockington (1903–2004) and the Revolution in Nurse-Education', *Journal of Medical Biography*, 16 (2008), 89–95.

Jones, A. E., and Metcalfe Brown, C. 'Screening for Cancer of the Cervix at Local Authority Clinics in Manchester', *The Lancet* (6 March 1965), 543.

Leeson, J. 'Health for All – Lessons from HIV/AIDS. Reflections of a Jobbing Public Health Doctor', *Public Health*, 105:1 (1991), 51–54.

Metcalfe Brown, C. 'The Officer of Health', *Public Health*, 60 (December 1946), 51–54.

——, 'The National Public Health Service', *Public Health*, 67 (October 1953), p.2.

Mottram, J. 'State Control in Local Context: Public Health and Midwifery Regulation in Manchester, 1900–1914', in H. Marland and A. M. Rafferty (eds), *Midwives, Society and Childbirth: Debates and Controversies in the Modern Period* (London: Routledge, 1997), pp. 134–52.

Perry, M. 'Academic General Practice in Manchester under the Early
    National Health Service: A Failed Experiment in Social Medicine',
    Journal of Social History of Medicine, 13:1 (2000), 111–129.
Pickstone, J. V. 'Dearth, Dirt and Fever Epidemics: Rewriting the History
    of British Public Health, 1780–1850', in T. Ranger and P. Slack (eds),
    Epidemics and Ideas: Essays on the Historical Perception of Pestilence
    (Cambridge: Cambridge University Press, 1992), 125–148.
——, 'Thomas Percival and the Production of Medical Ethics', in
    R. Baker, D. Porter and R. Porter (eds), *The Codification of Medical
    Morality* (Amsterdam: Kluwer Academic Publications, 1993), pp.161–178.
——, 'Medicine in Manchester: Manchester in Medicine, 1750–2005',
    Bulletin of the John Rylands University Library of Manchester, 87:1 (2005),
    13–42.
——, and Butler, S. V. F. 'The Politics of Medicine in the Early Industrial
    City: A Study of Hospital Reform and Medical Relief in Late
    Eighteenth-Century Manchester', *Medical History*, 28 (1984), 227–249.
Platt, H. L. 'From Hygeia to the Garden City: Bodies, Houses, and the
    Re-discovery of the Slum in Manchester, 1875–1910', *Journal of Urban
    History*, 35:5 (2002), 756–772.
Pooley, M. E., and Pooley, C. G. 'Health, Society and Environment in
    Victorian Manchester', in R. Woods and J. Woodward (eds), *Urban
    Disease and Mortality in Nineteenth-Century England* (London: Batsford
    Academic and Educational Ltd, 1984), pp.148–175.
Shapley. P. 'Tenants Arise! Consumerism, Tenants and the challenge of
    Council Authority in Manchester, 1968–92', *Social History*, 31:1 (2006),
    60–78.
——, Tanner, D., and Walling, A. 'Civic Culture and Housing Policy in
    Manchester, 1945–1979', *Twentieth-Century British History*, 15:4 (2004),
    410–434.
Toon, E. '"Cancer as the General Population Knows It": Knowledge, Fear,
    and Lay Education in 1950s Britain', *Bulletin of the History of Medicine*,
    81:1 (2007), 116–138.
Topping, A. 'Maternal Mortality and Public Opinion', *Public Health*, 49
    (July 1936), 342–349.
——, 'Prevention – Medical and Economic. Presidential Address to the
    Society of Medical Officers of Health, London, 17 September 1952',
    Public Health (November 1952), 16–17.
Walker, E. H. 'The Manchester School of Public Health, Abridgement of
    Presidential Address to the North-Western Branch of Medical Officers
    of Health', *Public Health*, 61 (December 1947), 39–40.

Unpublished Theses
Barclay, J. 'Langho Epileptic Colony, 1906–1984: A Contextual Study of
    the Origins, Transformations and Demise of Manchester's Colony for
    Sane Pauper Epileptics', University of Manchester Ph.D. Thesis (1988).

Harrington, V. 'Voices Beyond the Asylum: A Post-War History of Mental Health Services in Manchester and Salford', University of Manchester Ph.D. Thesis (2008).

Heggie, V. 'Re-imagining the Healthy Social Body: Medicine, Welfare and Health Reform in Manchester, 1880–1910', University of Manchester Ph.D. Thesis (2004).

Mottram, J. 'The Life and Work of John Roberton MRCS LSA, (1797–1876)', University of Manchester Institute of Science and Technology M.Sc. Thesis (1973).

Wilson, A. 'Technology and Municipal Decision-Making: Sanitary Systems in Manchester, 1868–1910', University of Manchester Ph.D. Thesis (1990).

Index

Page numbers in *italics* refer to illustrations
Page numbers in **bold** refer to biographical notes

Thatcher, Margaret and
    government, 56, 58, 72, 74,
    86–87
Thresh, J.C., 18
Topping, Andrew, 42–43
tuberculosis (TB), 2, 20, 22–25,
    27–28, 38, 41, 70–71, 112

University Teaching Health Centre,
    44, 47–48
University of Manchester, 1–2, 14,
    19–20, 26, 30–31, 33, 38–39,
    41–51, 54, 57, 61–62, 66, 70,
    81–85, 88, 97–101, 110–111, 121,
    124–126

VD. *See* venereal disease
Veitch Clark, R., 25–26, 38
venereal disease (VD), 20, 24, 41,
    118

Victoria University, 20. *See also*
    University of Manchester

Wanless, Sir Derek, 104
Wanless Reports, The, 104, 122
water-carriage system, 15, 17, 116
Watkins, Stephen, 114, **133**
Well Men Clinic, 64
Well Woman Clinic, 64–65, 74, 112
White, Charles, 7
WHO. *See* World Health
    Organisation
women's health, 7, 24, 29, 31, 36,
    38–39, 42, 47–48, 52, 54, 61,
    64–66, 69, 74, 84, 105–106, 112,
    116
workhouse hospitals, 10
World Health Organisation
    (WHO), 43, 50, 61–62, 94
Wythenshawe estate, 24, 25, 75, 96